POEMS IN HONOR OF AFRICAN HEROES AND LIBERATION LEADERS

David Saccoh Wright
Poems in Honor of African Heroes and Liberation Leaders

Published by Spines
ISBN: 979-8-89383-458-1

POEMS IN HONOR OF AFRICAN HEROES AND LIBERATION LEADERS

A BLUEPRINT FOR GOOD LEADERSHIP IN AFRICA

DAVID SACCOH WRIGHT

CONTENTS

ABOUT THE AUTHOR

David Saccoh Wright is a seasoned professional with a rich background in international affairs and a deep commitment to global development and peace. A proud alumnus of Ohio University, David holds a Master's degree in International Affairs, a testament to his academic prowess and dedication to understanding the complexities of global diplomacy and cooperation. His career began at the United Nations Development

Programme (UNDP), where he provided invaluable support to the Assistant Administrator's office within the Operations Support Group. His expertise and potential were quickly recognized, and David transitioned to the UN Secretariat as a Dutch-funded Junior Professional Officer. In this role, he contributed significantly to the Office of the Special Coordinator for Africa and Least Developed Countries, showcasing his dedication to some of the world's most vulnerable regions.

Over two decades at the United Nations have seen David evolve into a seasoned communicator and advocate within the Department of Global Communications. His work has been pivotal in shaping the narrative around the UN's mission and values, reaching out to diverse audiences worldwide. In addition, his tenure in the Department of Political and Peacebuilding Affairs has been marked by his support for conflict prevention initiatives in Africa, reflecting his unwavering commitment to fostering stability and peace on the continent.

Currently, David serves in the United Nations Office of the Special Adviser on Africa, where his focus on peace, security, and development issues continues to make a significant impact. His work is instrumental in driving forward the UN's agenda for a more peaceful and prosperous Africa, aligning with the broader goals of sustainable development and international cooperation.

Beyond his professional endeavors, David's passion for writing and mentorship shines through. He is deeply invested in guiding the youth, offering wisdom and encouragement as they navigate the complexities of life. His efforts bring a sense of hope and direction to the next generation, empowering them to build a brighter future.

As the United Nations prepares for the Summit of the Future in September 2024, David's involvement is anticipated to be a driving force in the event's success. His experience, insights, and dedication are sure to contribute to the summit's objectives, furthering the global discourse on how we can collectively forge a path toward a more equitable and sustainable world. David Saccoh Wright's legacy is one of impactful service, thoughtful leadership, and an enduring passion for making a difference in the lives of others, particularly in the realm of international affairs and development.

INTRODUCTION AND CONTEXT

In the intricate tapestry of Africa's history, the echoes of slavery and the struggle for independence from colonial powers resonate with profound significance. From the shackles of oppression to the dawn of freedom, the continent has endured a tumultuous journey, marked by imperialism's grip and the harsh realities of globalization's unequal embrace.

Amidst this complex narrative, the exploitation of natural resources has been a recurring theme, with external shocks often dictating the price of essential minerals, leaving African economies vulnerable to the whims of distant markets. Moreover, the scourge of bad governance and corruption has plagued the region, as leaders prioritize personal enrichment over the welfare of their people, perpetuating endemic poverty and a dearth of basic social services.

Tragically, the consequences of such systemic failures reverberate throughout society, with the youth, in particular, bearing the brunt of unemployment and disenfranchisement. In desperation, some turn to terrorism as a means of survival, further destabilizing regions already grappling with internal strife.

Yet, amidst these challenges, the imperative for good leadership and effective governance shines ever brighter. The need for strong states capable of delivering for their people is paramount, especially as climate change exacerbates existing vulnerabilities, as witnessed in recent catastrophic floods.

As we confront these realities, the call for unity through regional integration grows louder. By harnessing collective strength, mobilizing domestic resources, and addressing illicit financial flows, African nations can forge a path toward sustainable development and resilience in the face of climate uncertainty.

Central to this vision is the recognition of youth as the cornerstone of Africa's future. Investment in education, particularly in Science, Technology, Engineering, and Math (STEM) fields, is essential to unlocking the continent's potential and navigating the complexities of the Fourth Industrial Revolution.

In the midst of political upheaval and uncertainty, the renewal of democratic processes becomes imperative. The rise of coup d'états and military interventions underscores the urgency of nurturing leaders who prioritize the common good and adhere to constitutional principles.

It is within this context that the book of poems emerges, offering a beacon of hope amidst the tumult. Through the lens of pan-Africanist freedom fighters and the struggles of the past, it seeks to inspire the next generation to embrace courage and resilience in the quest for a brighter tomorrow.

The struggle for independence in Africa was championed by a number of remarkable leaders who fought against colonialism. Notable among them were Kwame Nkrumah of Ghana, who led his country to be the first sub-Saharan nation to gain independence; Jomo Kenyatta of Kenya, a key figure in the transition from British colonial rule to independence; Julius Nyerere of Tanzania, who promoted African socialism and unity; Léopold Sédar Senghor of Senegal, who was also a celebrated poet and cultural theorist; and Patrice Lumumba of the Democratic Republic of Congo, whose leadership and subsequent assassination became a symbol of the struggle against imperialism.

Africa's history is also replete with great kings and heroes who left indelible marks on the continent's history. Among many are Mansa Musa of Mali, known for his immense wealth and the flourishing of the Mali Empire under his rule; Shaka Zulu of the Zulu Kingdom, a military genius who united numerous Nguni tribes; Queen Nzinga of Ndongo and Matamba, who was known for her diplomatic and military skills in resisting Portuguese colonization; and Haile Selassie of Ethiopia, who became an emblematic figure for Pan-Africanists.

These leaders and monarchs are just a few examples of the many individuals who have shaped Africa's rich and diverse history. Their legacies continue to inspire and influence the continent and the world at large. Africa's past is not just a tale of colonization and struggle, but also one of resilience, innovation, and profound cultural achievements. The continent's history is a tapestry woven with the stories of these and many other leaders, each contributing to the complex and vibrant pattern that makes up Africa's identity. Their stories are a testament to the enduring spirit and the unyielding strength of the African people.

As we reflect on Africa's journey, let us heed the wisdom of those who came before, and in their footsteps, march towards a future defined by justice, prosperity, and the unyielding spirit of the African people.

BOOK OF POEMS

Kwame Nkrumah of Ghana

Kwame Nkrumah was a visionary leader and a driving force in Ghana's independence from British colonial rule. Born in September 1909 in Nkroful, Gold Coast (now Ghana), Nkrumah's early education was at a Roman Catholic elementary school, followed by Achimota College. His quest for knowledge led him to the United States, where he attended Lincoln University in Pennsylvania, earning master's degrees from both Lincoln and the University of Pennsylvania. During his time in the U.S., Nkrumah was influenced by the works of Karl Marx, Vladimir Lenin, and Marcus Garvey, shaping his ideologies around socialism and African nationalism.

Nkrumah's political activism intensified when he organized the 5th Pan-African Congress in Manchester, England, in 1945. Upon his return to the Gold Coast, he became the general secretary of the United Gold Coast Convention (UGCC), mobilizing the masses for self-governance. His efforts culminated in Ghana's independence in 1957, with Nkrumah as the first Prime Minister and later the first President when Ghana became a republic in 1960. His tenure was marked by significant achievements, including the establishment of numerous schools and universities, industrialization projects, and health facilities. Nkrumah was a staunch advocate for Pan-Africanism, striving for a united and self-sufficient Africa.

However, his presidency was not without controversy. His government faced challenges such as economic difficulties and accusations of authoritarianism. In 1966, Nkrumah's government was overthrown in a coup while he was abroad. Despite this, his legacy as a leader in the decolonization of Africa and his role in the formation of the Organization of African Unity (OAU) remain indelible. Nkrumah passed away on April 27, 1972, in Bucharest, Romania, but his vision and achievements continue to inspire generations in Ghana and across Africa.

In a land where cocoa beans dance in the sun,
Stood a man with a vision, second to none.
Kwame Nkrumah, a name we revere,
A leader, a dreamer, without any fear.

Born in Nkroful, where tales intertwine,
His journey began with a spark so divine.
From Catholic schools to Achimota's halls,
His quest for knowledge never stalls.

Crossing oceans to the land of the free,
In Pennsylvania, he found his decree.
With Marx, Lenin, and Garvey's embrace,
He crafted a path, a powerful grace.

Back in Ghana, he stirred up the fight,
For independence, under the African light.
Through speeches and congress, he led the way,
Ghana's freedom, a dawn's new day.

Prime Minister, President, titles he wore,
With industrial dreams, he aimed to soar.
Schools, hospitals, and factories too,
His legacy shines, bright and true.

But controversy brewed, challenges arose,
Economic woes and political throes.
Yet his spirit lives on, in every heart,
A beacon of hope, never to depart.

If Nkrumah were here, what would he do?
In today's world, with struggles anew?
He'd rally for unity, across every land,
African pride, hand in hand.

So let's heed his call, men of today,
Embrace his vision, in every way.
Make black men proud, in all that we do,
For Nkrumah's dream, lives on in you.

Jomo Kenyatta of Kenya

Jomo Kenyatta, born circa 1897, was a pivotal figure in Kenya's journey to independence and served as the nation's first President from 1964 until his death in 1978. His early political engagement began with the Kikuyu Central Association, where he fought for the rights of the Kikuyu people, particularly against the seizure of their lands after Kenya became part of the British Empire in 1920. Kenyatta's proficiency in English led to his role as the general secretary of the KCA, allowing him to amplify anti-colonial sentiments and advocate for fair land rights. His efforts extended to the international stage, where he represented Kikuyu interests in London and co-organized the Fifth Pan-African Congress in 1945. As President of the Kenya African Union, he was instrumental in the struggle for Kenya's independence from Britain. Kenyatta's leadership saw the establishment of agencies to assist indigenous Kenyans, the abolition of colonial laws allowing racial discrimination, and significant educational reforms. He also played a crucial role in Kenya's foreign policy, overseeing its entry into the United Nations and fostering trade agreements with neighboring countries, while maintaining a pro-Western, anti-Communist stance. His tenure was marked by stability, which attracted foreign investment and contributed to Kenya's development. Kenyatta's legacy is multifaceted, as he is celebrated for his contributions to Kenya's independence and criticized for his subsequent authoritarian rule.

In the land of Kenya, long ago,
Lived a man named Jomo, don't you know?
Born in the late 1800s, he was,
A leader who caused quite the buzz.

With a twinkle in his eye and a pen in hand,
He fought for justice across the land.
From the Kikuyu Central Association, he rose,
To challenge oppression, his courage shows.

Against colonial rule, he took a stand,
For the rights of his people, he had a plan.
Representing Kenya on the global stage,
He stirred hearts with passion, wisdom, and rage.

In London's halls, his voice rang clear,
Demanding justice for all to hear.
Co-organizing Pan-African dreams,
Stitching together liberation's seams.

As Kenya's first President, he led the way,
Through trials and triumphs, come what may.
Establishing agencies, abolishing laws,
He championed progress, without pause.

In foreign affairs, he held his ground,
A voice for Kenya, profound and sound.
Welcoming trade, fostering peace,
His leadership brought Kenya release.

But if Jomo were with us today,
What would he do, what would he say?
Perhaps he'd urge us to unite,
To fight for justice with all our might.

To emulate his spirit bold,
In every story yet untold.
To stand for truth, to fight the fight,
And make black men proud with all our might.

So let's raise a toast to Jomo Kenyatta's name,
A leader of courage, a man of acclaim.
May his legacy inspire us anew,
To build a better world for me and you.

Julius Mwalimu Nyerere of Tanzania

Julius Nyerere, known affectionately as Mwalimu or "Teacher," was a pivotal figure in Tanzanian history and African politics. Born in April 1922 in Butiama, he was the first Tanzanian to study at a British university, earning a Master's degree in history and economics from the University of Edinburgh. As a visionary leader, he became the first Prime Minister of independent Tanganyika in 1961 and later served as the first President of Tanzania from 1964 to 1985. Nyerere was instrumental in the formation of the Organization of African Unity, now known as the African Union. His political ideology,

Ujamaa, was a form of African socialism that emphasized cooperative agriculture, equality, and self-reliance, which he detailed in the Arusha Declaration. Under his leadership, Tanzania implemented the collectivization of village farmlands, mass literacy campaigns, and free and universal education. He was also a key figure in the liberation movements of southern Africa and a proponent of peaceful change and racial harmony.

Nyerere's tenure saw significant strides in uniting diverse ethnic groups, promoting a single national language, Swahili, and fostering a sense of Tanzanian national identity. His efforts in education led to a dramatic increase in literacy rates and access to education for Tanzanians. Internationally, he was recognized with awards such as the Lenin Peace Prize and the Gandhi Peace Prize for his contributions to peace and international cooperation. Despite facing criticism for some of his policies, particularly the economic challenges that arose from his socialist programs, Nyerere's legacy as a teacher, statesman, and advocate for African unity and development remains influential. His commitment to social equality and his role in shaping Tanzania's post-colonial identity are celebrated, and his philosophical contributions continue to be studied and admired globally.

In the heart of Tanzania's history, stands tall,
A figure revered, Mwalimu Nyerere, above all.
With wisdom and wit, he led the way,
In shaping a nation, come what may.

Born in Butiama, a land of dreams,
His vision stretched far, like flowing streams.
From Edinburgh's halls, he brought back the light,
To guide his people, day and night.

Ujamaa's call echoed, loud and clear,
"Cooperation and equality" we'll hold dear.
In fields and classrooms, his teachings spread,
Uniting a nation, where hope was fed.

As President and teacher, he wore many hats,
Championing peace, despite the spats.
With Swahili's embrace, a language so dear,
He bridged divides, year after year.

Now if Nyerere were still around,
In the world's stage, he'd surely astound.
Promoting unity, amidst chaos and strife,
Urging for peace, to enrich life.

Men of today, take heed and learn,
From Mwalimu's legacy, let it burn.
Embrace education, strive for unity,
And make your ancestors proud, with dignity.

For in Nyerere's footsteps, greatness lies,
In serving others, the ultimate prize.
So let's emulate his grace and might,
And make black men proud, in every light.

Léopold Sédar Senghor of Senegal

Léopold Sédar Senghor was a seminal figure in African history, renowned for his multifaceted contributions to politics, literature, and philosophy. Born on October 9, 1906, in Joal, Senegal, Senghor rose from humble beginnings to become the first president of Senegal, serving from 1960 to 1980. His political journey began with his election as a deputy to the French National Assembly in 1946, where he advocated for the rights of African territories within the French Union. Senghor's vision for Senegal was rooted in the philosophy of

Négritude, a concept he co-developed to celebrate African culture and identity. As a statesman, Senghor was instrumental in achieving Senegalese independence and later established the Senegalese Democratic Bloc. His tenure as president was marked by the promotion of African socialism and the fostering of French-African ties. Despite facing political challenges, including a fallout with Prime Minister Mamadou Dia, Senghor's leadership was pivotal in maintaining stability and progress in post-colonial Senegal.

Senghor's achievements extend beyond politics into the realms of education and literature. He was the first African to attain the prestigious agrégé qualification in France, allowing him to teach at the highest levels of the French educational system. His literary prowess was recognized with his election as the first African member of the Académie française. Senghor's poetry and writings, deeply influenced by his Négritude philosophy, have left an indelible mark on French and Senegalese literature. His legacy is honored through various recognitions, including honorary degrees and the naming of institutions after him. The Léopold Sédar Senghor International Airport in Dakar stands as a testament to his enduring influence. Senghor's dedication to the upliftment of African identity and his contributions to fostering a sense of pride among African peoples are celebrated globally. His death on December 20, 2001, marked the end of an era, but his achievements continue to inspire future generations.

In Joal, on the ninth of October born,
Léopold Sédar Senghor, from dawn to morn,
A titan of Africa, in history renowned,
In politics, literature, and thought profound.

From humble roots, he soared on high,
To lead his nation, reach for the sky.
As Senegal's first president, he stood tall,
Guiding his people through each rise and fall.

In '46, to the French Assembly, he went,
With eloquent words, his people's rights he meant.
Négritude, his philosophy, bold and clear,
Celebrating Africa's culture dear.

Independence he fought for, a nation's dream,
With socialism's ideals, a bright gleam.
Through trials and triumphs, he led the way,
In Senegal's story, a shining ray.

Teaching in France, his wisdom spread,
In Académie française, his words led.
Poetry flowed from his pen's might,
A beacon for Africa's cultural fight.

If Senghor walked among us today,
He'd champion unity in every way.
Encouraging pride in black men's name,
Building bridges, not fueling flame.

In his legacy, men of today should find,
A call to uplift all of humankind.
Embrace diversity, foster unity's art,
And let Senghor's spirit live in every heart.

Patrice Lumumba of the Democratic Republic of Congo

Patrice Lumumba was a central figure in the history of the Democratic Republic of Congo (DRC), remembered for his passionate pursuit of independence for his country from Belgian colonial rule. Born on July 2, 1925, in Onalua, Belgian Congo, Lumumba emerged as a fervent nationalist and a charismatic leader. He was instrumental in the struggle that led to the Congo's independence on June 30, 1960, and subsequently became the country's first democratically elected Prime Minister. Lumumba's tenure as Prime Minister was short-lived, from June to September 1960, but his impact was profound. He was a pioneer in advocating for pan-Africanism and sought to unite the diverse ethnic groups within the Congo under a single national identity. His vision was for a modern, democratic state free from the influence of colonial powers and the exploitation of its natural resources by foreign entities.

Despite his efforts, Lumumba's administration faced immediate challenges, including a mutiny within the army and secessionist movements in the mineral-rich province of Katanga. The political crisis that ensued led to his dismissal from office and eventually to his tragic assassination on January 17, 1961, an event that sent shockwaves throughout the African continent and the world. Lumumba's legacy is marked by his eloquent speeches and writings, which articulated the aspirations of the Congolese people and the broader African liberation movement. He is celebrated for his unwavering commitment to sovereignty and social justice, which inspired many future African leaders. His life and work have been extensively studied, and he is often cited as a symbol of resistance against oppression and a martyr for the cause of African independence.

In recognition of his contributions, Lumumba's image and ideals continue to resonate in contemporary Congolese politics and culture. His name and memory are honored in various ways, including streets, stadiums, and institutions bearing his name, ensuring that his vision for the Congo lives on. Despite the controversies that surrounded his political career and his untimely death, Patrice Lumumba remains a towering figure in the pantheon of African nationalists and a beacon of hope for a united and prosperous Africa.

In the heart of Congo, where tales unfold,
Lived a man of courage, strong and bold.
Patrice Lumumba, a name revered,
In the fight for freedom, he persevered.

Born under colonial skies, he arose,
With dreams of liberty, breaking oppression's throes.
From Onalua's embrace to the world's stage,
His passion ignited, with wisdom and rage.

July 2, 1925, the date of his birth,
A leader destined to alter the Earth.
Charismatic and bold, his voice did resound,
For Congo's independence, he tirelessly wound.

June 30, 1960, a historic day,
When Congo's chains began to fray.
Elected Prime Minister, his dream took flight,
To lead his people toward the light.

But challenges loomed, as shadows do,
Mutinies and secession, a turbulent brew.
Yet Lumumba stood tall, in the face of strife,
For his vision of unity, he'd give his life.

In modern times, if Lumumba were here,
He'd champion justice, dispel all fear.
Uniting nations, fostering peace,
His legacy's reach would only increase.

Men of today, in every land,
Can heed his call, take a stand.
Embrace his spirit, his passion ignite,
And strive for justice, with all their might.

For Lumumba's legacy, a guiding star,
A beacon of hope, no matter how far.
In his footsteps, may men proudly tread,
And honor his memory, long after he's fled.

So let us remember, with joy and pride,
Patrice Lumumba, our Congolese guide.
His name lives on, in history's embrace,
A symbol of courage, for every race.

Mansa Musa of Mali

Mansa Musa, also known as Musa I of Mali, was the ruler of the Mali Empire from 1312 to 1337. He is celebrated for his immense wealth and his significant contributions to the Islamic world and West Africa. His achievements include expanding the Mali Empire to include a large part of West Africa, establishing Timbuktu as a center of trade and Islamic learning, and embarking on a famous pilgrimage to Mecca in 1324, which showcased his wealth and generosity. Mansa Musa's reign saw the construction of numerous mosques and madrasas, particularly the legendary Djinguereber Mosque in Timbuktu, which became a jewel of Islamic architecture. He also initiated and fostered diplomatic and economic relations with other states and empires, further increasing Mali's wealth and influence. His pilgrimage to Mecca, during which he distributed gold so lavishly that it disrupted the economy of the regions he passed through, left a lasting impression on the world, highlighting the Mali Empire's prosperity and Musa's devoutness. Mansa Musa's legacy endures in the rich manuscripts, educational institutions, and architectural wonders that continue to stand as testaments to a golden age of Mali's history.

In Mali's realm, a tale unfurls,
Of Mansa Musa, with his golden swirls.
From Timbuktu's sands to Mecca's glow,
His wealth and wisdom, they did flow.

A ruler rich beyond compare,
With gold to spare and jewels to wear.
He built mosques tall, with minarets high,
A legacy that reaches the sky.

In Timbuktu, he made his mark,
With learning and trade, he left his spark.
Djinguereber Mosque, a shining gem,
A beacon of faith, for all to stem.

On pilgrimage, his caravan did tread,
With gold so much, it turned heads.
In Mecca's heart, he bowed his head,
His faith and wealth, no words unsaid.

But if Mansa Musa walked today,
What would he do, what would he say?
Perhaps he'd urge us to follow his lead,
To strive for greatness, in word and deed.

To build, to learn, to spread our wealth,
To nurture minds, to foster health.
To bridge divides, with open hands,
And lift our brothers from distant lands.

So let us emulate this king of old,
With hearts of gold, and stories bold.
And make our ancestors' hearts sing loud,
As we walk in their footsteps, tall and proud.

Shaka Zulu of the Zulu Kingdom

Shaka Zulu, born circa 1787, was a significant figure in the history of Southern Africa, renowned for his military innovations and leadership that led to the creation of the Zulu Empire. As the chief of the Zulus from 1816 to 1828, he transformed his initially small and insignificant tribe into a formidable force. Shaka's early life was marked by rejection and hardship due to the irregular marriage of his parents, which violated Zulu customs. Despite these challenges, he rose to prominence as a warrior under the Mthethwa Empire's paramount chieftain, Dingiswayo. Upon his father's death, Shaka assumed leadership of the Zulu and immediately began reorganizing the army. He introduced the short-hafted stabbing spear, known as the assegai, compelling his warriors to engage in close combat, which revolutionized traditional warfare methods. Shaka also implemented a regimental system based on age groups, with distinct markings for identification, fostering unity and discipline among his troops. His military campaigns were highly effective, significantly expanding the Zulu territory and influence. Shaka's reign coincided with the Mfecane, a period of widespread chaos and warfare in the region, and his actions contributed to the reshaping of the region's demographic and political landscape. His legacy is complex, with some viewing him as a ruthless leader, while others recognize his genius in state-building and military strategy. Shaka's assassination in 1828 by his half-brothers ended his influential yet controversial rule. His impact on Zulu culture and the broader history of South Africa remains a subject of study and debate.

In the heart of Africa, long ago,
Lived a man named Shaka, don't you know?
Born amidst customs, tangled and tight,
But destined to shine with warrior might.

In eighteen hundred and twenty-eight,
Shaka ruled, his kingdom great.
From humble roots, he did ascend,
To lead the Zulus, a chief to commend.

With spear in hand and strategy keen,
He carved out realms where once was seen
But scattered tribes, now unified,
Under Shaka's banner, they marched in stride.

His assegai swift, his army bold,
In close combat, their story told.
A regimental force, disciplined and strong,
From his leadership, they did belong.

But if Shaka lived in modern days,
How would he tread life's tricky maze?
Perhaps he'd coach a rugby team,
With tactics sharp, fulfilling his dream.

Or maybe he'd be a CEO,
Leading with prowess, making the dough.
In boardrooms fierce, his presence felt,
A modern-day chief, where deals are dealt.

Yet, amidst success and worldly gain,
Shaka's lessons would still remain.
Unity, discipline, and strength untold,
In every endeavor, his legacy bold.

So, men of today, take heed and learn,
From Shaka's tale, let your fire burn.
Embrace your roots, stand tall and proud,
With courage and honor, let your voice be loud.

For Shaka Zulu, though long gone,
His spirit lives and carries on.
In every heart that dares to fight,
For justice, truth, and what is right.

Queen Nzinga of Ndongo and Matamba

Queen Nzinga of Ndongo and Matamba, also known as Njinga Mbande, was a remarkable ruler in the 17th century, whose achievements were significant in the history of Angola. Born around 1583, she was a member of the ruling family of Ndongo and demonstrated an early aptitude for political and military strategies. Upon her brother's death in 1624, she ascended to the throne of Ndongo during a period of conflict and the burgeoning African slave trade. Nzinga is renowned for her diplomatic wisdom, particularly in her negotiations with the Portuguese, which were aimed at preserving the sovereignty of her people. She was a formidable military leader, who, after facing setbacks, allied with the Imbangala warlord Kasanje to rebuild her forces and subsequently took control of the Kingdom of Matamba, establishing herself as queen from 1631 to 1663.

Her reign was marked by her astute leadership and military prowess, as she led her kingdom through periods of Portuguese encroachment and conflict. Nzinga made alliances with foreign powers, such as the Dutch West India Company, to resist Portuguese colonization efforts. Despite suffering losses, including the recapture of Luanda by the Portuguese in 1648, she continued to resist until a peace treaty was signed in 1656. Nzinga's ability to transform Matamba into a commercial powerhouse, rivaling Portuguese colonies, was one of her notable achievements. She was also skilled in espionage and warfare tactics, which she used to safeguard her territories well into her sixties.

Nzinga's legacy extends beyond her military and political feats; she is celebrated for her intelligence and her role as a symbol of resistance against colonialism. Her leadership helped to shape the identity and history of Angola, making her a revered figure in the Atlantic Creole culture. The establishment of a new capital in Matamba and strategic alliances that bolstered her kingdom's defense are testaments to her ruling prowess.

Nzinga's battles, such as the Battle of Senga and the victory at Ilamba, showcased her military acumen against formidable Portuguese forces. Her life and reign are a testament to her enduring spirit and her unwavering commitment to her people's freedom and autonomy. Queen Nzinga's story is a powerful narrative of resilience, leadership, and the struggle for sovereignty in the face of colonial expansion.

In Angola's annals, a queen did reign,
Nzinga, a legend, forever shall remain.
Born to lead, with a wit so keen,
In the 17th century, a formidable queen.

With her brother's demise, she took the throne,
In a land where power struggles were widely known.
Facing Portuguese encroachment, she stood tall,
Crafting alliances, she answered the call.

Diplomatic prowess, a masterful art,
She negotiated with a cunning heart.
Preserving her people's sovereignty,
In the face of colonial animosity.

But Nzinga wasn't just a diplomat, you see,
Her military genius set her people free.
She allied with Kasanje, a warrior bold,
Rebuilt her forces, her story to unfold.

Matamba's queen, her reign did soar,
Commercial prowess, like never before.
Spycraft and warfare, her tools of trade,
In her sixties, still, she never strayed.

If Nzinga walked among us today,
Her wisdom and strength would light the way.
For women, especially, her tale does inspire,
To stand firm, to reach higher and higher.

In every battle, in every strife,
To fight for justice, to live with life.
To emulate Nzinga, is to proudly stand,
With unwavering resolve, across the land.

So let her story echo loud and clear,
A beacon of hope for all to hear.
For in her legacy, we find our guide,
To honor our past, with every stride.

Queen Cleopatra VII of Egypt

Queen Cleopatra VII, the last monarch of the Ptolemaic dynasty, was a ruler of remarkable ability and charisma, whose life and legacy have captivated historians and the public alike. Ascending to the throne at the tender age of 18, she quickly demonstrated her acumen by stabilizing Egypt's economy and skillfully navigating the treacherous waters of Roman politics. Cleopatra was a polyglot, fluent in multiple languages, which aided her in diplomatic negotiations and in maintaining her power. Her strategic alliance and romantic liaisons with Julius Caesar and later Mark

Antony were pivotal in her efforts to preserve Egypt's independence from Rome. Cleopatra's reign saw the consolidation of her rule in Egypt, and she was revered as the earthly embodiment of the goddess Isis, which bolstered her standing among her subjects. Her influence extended beyond politics to the arts and fashion, leaving an indelible mark on the culture of the time. Despite her efforts, after the defeat at the Battle of Actium and the subsequent loss of her allies, Cleopatra's life ended in tragedy, marking the end of an era and the beginning of Roman dominion over Egypt. Her achievements, however, from her diplomatic prowess to her cultural patronage, continue to be celebrated as a testament to her enduring impact on history.

Cleopatra VII, the queen of sass,
With wit as sharp as cut glass.
She ruled Egypt with grace and flair,
With style and charm beyond compare.

At eighteen, she took the throne,
And from then on, she was known
For her savvy in politics and love,
As fierce as a lioness from above.

A polyglot, she spoke with ease,
In tongues that made her enemies freeze.
Her alliances with Caesar and Antony,
Brought Egypt fame and victory.

But imagine if Cleo were here today,
What mischief and brilliance would she display?
Perhaps she'd be ruling a tech empire,
Or dazzling us all on a stage as a fire.

Women of today, take heed and learn,
From Cleopatra's legacy, let it burn.
Be bold, be smart, be unapologetically you,
And watch as your dreams and ambitions come true.

In Cleopatra's footsteps, let us stride,
With confidence and grace by our side.
For she made history proud and loud,
A queen like her, we should all be proud.

Haile Selassie of Ethiopia

Haile Selassie I, born Tafari Makonnen on July 23, 1892, was the Emperor of Ethiopia from 1930 to 1974. He is remembered for his efforts to modernize Ethiopia and for his significant role in international politics during the post-World War II era. Selassie brought Ethiopia into the League of Nations and later the United Nations, making Addis Ababa a central hub for the Organization of African Unity, now known as the African Union. His governance was marked by attempts to modernize the country through political and social reforms, including the introduction of Ethiopia's first written constitution and the abolition of slavery.

Educated by French missionaries, Selassie was an intellectual who impressed Emperor Menelik II with his abilities, leading to his rapid rise in government. As governor of Sidamo and Harer, he sought to weaken the feudal nobility and strengthen central governance. His marriage to Wayzaro Menen, a descendant of Menelik II, solidified his position within the royal family. After Menelik II's death, Selassie became a key political figure, eventually ascending to the throne after deposing Lij Yasu and serving as regent for Empress Zauditu.

Internationally, Selassie was recognized for his diplomatic skills, becoming an advocate for pan-Africanism and playing a pivotal role in the decolonization of Africa. He was a founding member of the United Nations and served as the chairperson of the Organisation of African Unity. His efforts extended to educational reforms, with the establishment of Ethiopia's first university, and to healthcare, with the construction of new hospitals. Despite his progressive policies, Selassie's reign was not without controversy. His government faced criticism for its handling of famine and for the autocratic elements of his rule. In 1974, he was deposed in a coup d'état, marking the end of the Solomonic dynasty's rule. Haile Selassie passed away on August 27, 1975, but his legacy as a reformer and a key figure in African politics endures.

In Ethiopia's annals, a legend arose,
A monarch whose tale in history flows.
Born Tafari Makonnen, with a regal air,
Haile Selassie I, beyond compare.

From 1930 to '74, he reigned supreme,
Crafting dreams and visions, like a poetic dream.
Modernizing Ethiopia, his noble quest,
To lift his people to their very best.

In League of Nations, his voice did resound,
At UN's doorstep, he was ever found.
Pan-Africanism, his fervent creed,
In unity, he saw Africa freed.

Educated by missionaries with grace,
Selassie's intellect, a dazzling embrace.
Rising swiftly, with each noble feat,
To governance, he brought a modern beat.

Married to Menen, a royal alliance strong,
Their love and unity, a lifelong song.
Reformer, diplomat, a beacon bright,
In Africa's journey, a guiding light.

Today, if Selassie walked among us still,
He'd champion causes with unwavering will.
From education to healthcare, his focus clear,
Empowering his people, banishing fear.

In his footsteps, men of today should tread,
With courage, wisdom, and hearts widespread.
Emulate his vision, his spirit true,
Making black men proud, in all they do.

Though his reign saw shadows and strife,
Haile Selassie's legacy, the essence of life.
A leader, a legend, forevermore,
In Ethiopia's heart, he'll eternally soar.

Nelson Mandela of South Africa

Nelson Mandela, the revered statesman of South Africa, stands as an emblem of courage, resilience, and reconciliation. Born on July 18, 1918, Mandela dedicated his life to the fight against apartheid, a system of institutionalized racial segregation that entrenched inequality in South Africa. A lawyer by profession, Mandela joined the African National Congress (ANC) in the 1940s, becoming increasingly involved in anti-apartheid activism. He played a key role in the ANC's defiance campaign and was a co-founder of its militant wing, Umkhonto we Sizwe (MK), in 1961. In 1962,

Mandela was arrested and sentenced to life imprisonment for his involvement in sabotage activities against the apartheid government. He spent 27 years behind bars, during which he became a symbol of the struggle for justice and equality, both domestically and internationally. Mandela's release from prison in 1990 marked a turning point in South Africa's history. His unwavering commitment to reconciliation and negotiation paved the way for the end of apartheid and the transition to democracy.

In 1994, Mandela became South Africa's first democratically elected black president, serving a single term until 1999. Among his notable achievements as president was the establishment of the Truth and Reconciliation Commission, which aimed to heal the wounds of apartheid by providing a platform for victims and perpetrators to confront the past. Mandela's leadership also focused on fostering national unity, promoting human rights, and advancing socio-economic development, particularly in marginalized communities. Internationally, Mandela was revered as a symbol of peace and justice. He received numerous awards, including the Nobel Peace Prize in 1993, for his efforts to dismantle apartheid and build a democratic and inclusive South Africa. Even after stepping down from the presidency, Mandela remained a global advocate for human rights, education, and HIV/AIDS awareness until his passing on December 5, 2013. His legacy continues to inspire people worldwide, reminding us of the power of forgiveness, reconciliation, and the pursuit of justice.

In South Africa's tapestry, a hero bold,
Nelson Mandela, with a spirit untold.
Courage, resilience, in him did reside,
Against apartheid's tide, he dared to stride.

Born in July's warmth, nineteen-eighteen,
To battle injustice, his soul keen.
A lawyer turned activist, a lion's roar,
In ANC's ranks, he waged his war.

With Umkhonto we Sizwe, he took a stand,
For freedom's cause, he raised his hand.
But '62 brought a fateful twist,
Behind bars, Mandela's courage persist.

Twenty-seven years in captivity's hold,
Yet Mandela's spirit could not be cold.
A beacon of hope, a symbol of might,
For justice and equality, he'd fight.

In '90, freedom's light did gleam,
Mandela's release, a liberation's dream.
Reconciliation, his guiding star,
Apartheid's end, a battle scar.

As president, his legacy soared,
Truth and Reconciliation, its sword.
Uniting a nation, healing its pain,
Mandela's leadership, a golden chain.

Now if Mandela walked among us today,
His voice would still lead, in every way.
Advocating for justice, equality's song,
Inspiriting hearts, righting every wrong.

Men of today, his footsteps trace,
With dignity, courage, and grace.
Emulate Mandela, make his legacy loud,
In every action, make black men proud.

For his spirit lives on, in every deed,
A beacon of hope, for those in need.
Nelson Mandela, a legend's embrace,
In history's hall, he finds his place.

Ahmed Sékou Touré of Guinea

Ahmed Sékou Touré was a pivotal figure in the struggle for independence and the subsequent governance of Guinea. Born on January 9, 1922, Touré rose to prominence as a leader of the Rassemblement Démocratique Africain (RDA), advocating for the rights of African colonies under French rule. After Guinea gained independence from France in 1958, Touré became the country's first president. He embarked on a mission to establish Guinea as a socialist state, implementing policies aimed at nationalizing key industries, promoting agrarian reform, and advocating for Pan-Africanism.

Under Touré's leadership, Guinea played a significant role in the Pan-African movement, supporting liberation struggles across the continent and fostering diplomatic ties with other African nations. He was a vocal critic of neocolonialism and imperialism, advocating for African unity and self-determination. Touré's regime, however, was marked by authoritarianism and political repression. Opposition parties were banned, dissent was stifled, and human rights abuses were widespread. Despite these challenges, Touré's government made strides in education and healthcare, significantly expanding access to these services for Guinean citizens.

Internationally, Touré's legacy is mixed. While he was celebrated as a champion of African independence and unity, his authoritarian rule and human rights violations drew criticism from international observers. Ahmed Sékou Touré passed away on March 26, 1984, leaving behind a complex legacy. His contributions to the struggle against colonialism and his efforts to promote African unity and socialism are remembered, alongside the challenges and controversies of his tenure as Guinea's leader.

In Guinea's story, a man of might,
Ahmed Sékou Touré, shining bright.
Born to lead, on January's day,
In Africa's heart, he'd find his way.

With RDA's banner, he took a stand,
For African rights, across the land.
Independence won, in '58's glow,
Touré's star rising, in freedom's flow.

As Guinea's first president, he'd soar,
Dreaming of socialism, his heart's core.
Nationalizing industries, with a flair,
In Pan-Africanism, he'd declare.

A critic of neocolonial might,
Touré fought on, for Africa's right.
In liberation's song, he'd lend his voice,
For unity, he'd fiercely rejoice.

Yet amid the cheers, a shadow crept,
In authoritarian ways, he'd adept.
Opposition banned, dissent oppressed,
A mix of progress and unrest.

But let's imagine Touré, alive today,
Leading with wisdom, come what may.
Advocating for justice, with all his might,
In education and healthcare's light.

Men of today, his legacy heed,
In leadership, in every deed.
Emulate his passion, his fight,
Make black men proud, in day and night.

For Touré's story, complex and grand,
A champion, with flaws on hand.
In Africa's tale, he finds his place,
A leader, a dreamer, in time's embrace.

Gamal Abdel Nasser of Egypt

Gamal Abdel Nasser, a towering figure in modern Egyptian history, was born on January 15, 1918. He emerged as a leader during the tumultuous period of post-colonial Egypt, spearheading significant political, social, and economic reforms. Nasser's rise to prominence began with his involvement in the Free Officers Movement, a group of nationalist military officers who sought to end British influence and corruption in Egypt. In 1952, Nasser played a central role in the overthrow of King Farouk and the establishment of the Egyptian Republic. As the de facto leader of Egypt, he served as Prime Minister and later as

President, consolidating power and implementing sweeping changes. Nasser's vision for Egypt was deeply rooted in Arab nationalism and socialism, with the goal of modernizing the country and asserting its independence on the world stage.

One of Nasser's most significant achievements was the nationalization of the Suez Canal in 1956, a move that challenged Western dominance in the region and symbolized Egypt's newfound assertiveness. Although the ensuing Suez Crisis resulted in military intervention by Britain, France, and Israel, Nasser's defiance garnered widespread support across the Arab world and solidified his status as a champion of anti-imperialism. Internally, Nasser embarked on ambitious land reforms, redistributing land from wealthy landowners to peasants in an effort to alleviate poverty and inequality. He also implemented social welfare programs, including the expansion of education and healthcare services, which significantly improved the living standards of ordinary Egyptians.

Nasser's leadership extended beyond Egypt's borders, as he emerged as a prominent leader of the Non-Aligned Movement and a key advocate for Arab unity. His efforts to unite the Arab world against colonialism and imperialism resonated across the region, earning him admiration and support from millions of people.

Despite his achievements, Nasser's legacy is not without controversy. His authoritarian rule and suppression of political dissent drew criticism from human rights groups, while his ambitious economic projects faced challenges and setbacks. Nevertheless, Nasser remains a revered figure in Egypt and the broader Arab world, remembered for his role in shaping the modern Middle East and his unwavering commitment to the cause of Arab nationalism and social justice.

In Egypt's annals, a legend's tale,
Of Nasser's wit, we gladly regale.
Born in January's winter chill,
A leader bold, with iron will.

From Free Officers' ranks he rose,
To challenge foes, to break the throes.
King Farouk ousted, Egypt anew,
Nasser's vision, strong and true.

With Arab nationalism, he'd soar,
Socialism's dream, his heart's core.
The Suez Canal, a bold decree,
Challenging powers, setting Egypt free.

In land reforms, he'd take a stand,
From wealthy hands to peasant's land.
Education, healthcare, for all to share,
Nasser's Egypt, beyond compare.

Non-Aligned Movement, his stage grand,
Uniting Arabs, across the sand.
Against imperialism, he'd fight,
With courage shining, in day and night.

But amid the cheers, a shadow cast,
His rule, at times, too firm and fast.
Dissent silenced, rights repressed,
A leader flawed, yet still, the best.

If Nasser walked among us today,
In Arab unity, he'd lead the way.
Advocating justice, with all his might,
In every action, in every fight.

Men of today, his spirit heed,
In leadership, in every deed.
Emulate his passion, his might,
Make black men proud, in day and night.

For Nasser's legacy, shines bright,
A beacon of hope, in darkest night.
In Egypt's heart, he finds his place,
A leader, a dreamer, in time's embrace.

Thomas Sankara of Burkina Faso

Thomas Sankara, often referred to as "Africa's Che Guevara," was a revolutionary leader and President of Burkina Faso. Born on December 21, 1949, Sankara emerged as a charismatic and visionary leader during a time of great social and political upheaval in Burkina Faso, then known as Upper Volta. Sankara rose to power through a military coup in 1983, overthrowing the government of President Jean-Baptiste Ouédraogo. As President, Sankara embarked on a radical transformation of Burkina Faso, with a vision of creating a truly independent and self-reliant nation.

One of Sankara's most notable achievements was his emphasis on grassroots mobilization and participatory democracy. He launched ambitious programs to empower women, including initiatives to promote gender equality, and access to education and healthcare. Sankara also implemented land reform measures aimed at redistributing land from feudal landlords to peasants, as well as nationalizing key industries to promote economic self-sufficiency.

In addition to his domestic reforms, Sankara was a staunch advocate for Pan-Africanism and African unity. He criticized foreign aid and debt dependency, calling for African nations to reject external influence and chart their own path to development. Sankara's leadership style was marked by simplicity and integrity. He famously eschewed the trappings of power, living modestly and refusing to accept lavish perks of office. His commitment to austerity and anti-corruption earned him admiration both within Burkina Faso and across the continent. Tragically, Sankara's tenure as President was cut short by a coup d'état in 1987, orchestrated by his close associate Blaise Compaoré. Sankara was assassinated at the age of 37, but his legacy continues to inspire generations of Africans. Today, Sankara is remembered as a symbol of anti-imperialism, social justice, and African liberation. His bold vision and unwavering commitment to the welfare of his people have cemented his place as one of Africa's most iconic leaders.

In Burkina Faso's tale, a hero arose,
Thomas Sankara, with a cheeky pose.
Born in December's winter glow,
A revolutionary spirit, all would know.

Through coup and clamor, he'd seize the throne,
A vision grand, all on his own.
Grassroots mobilization, his creed,
Empowering women, with lightning speed.

Gender equality, education's call,
Sankara's vision, breaking down the wall.
Land reform, from feudal chains unbound,
Peasants rejoicing, in freedom's sound.

Nationalizing industries, he'd proclaim,
Economic self-sufficiency, his aim.
Pan-Africanism, his heart's song,
Rejecting foreign aid, righting every wrong.

Simplicity, integrity, his guiding light,
In modesty, he'd find his might.
No trappings of power, for this man,
Austerity, his lifelong plan.

But alas, his reign, cut short by fate,
A coup d'état, sealing his state.
Assassinated, in his prime,
Yet his legacy, a beacon's shine.

If Sankara walked among us today,
In African unity, he'd lead the way.
Advocating justice, with all his might,
In every action, in every fight.

Men of today, his spirit heed,
In leadership, in every deed.
Emulate his passion, his might,
Make black men proud, in day and night.

For Sankara's legacy, still ablaze,
In hearts and minds, through endless days.
A symbol of justice, of liberation's art,
Thomas Sankara, forever in our heart.

Joseph Jenkins Roberts of Liberia

Joseph Jenkins Roberts, born on March 15, 1809, in Norfolk, Virginia, was a pioneering figure in African-American history. As an Americo-Liberian merchant, he emigrated to Liberia in 1829 and became a prominent politician. His most notable achievement was becoming the first and seventh president of Liberia, serving from 1848 to 1856 and again from 1872 to 1876. Roberts was instrumental in Liberia's journey to independence and was the first person of African descent to govern the country. Before his presidency, he served as the governor of Liberia from 1841 to 1848. His leadership was pivotal during the early years of the nation's formation, where he worked tirelessly to establish Liberia's sovereignty, secure foreign recognition, and lay the foundations for its future. His efforts culminated in Liberia's declaration of independence in 1847, and under his guidance, the new republic was recognized by major powers such as Great Britain and other European nations. Roberts' legacy extends beyond his political achievements; he was also a key figure in the establishment of Liberia College and served as its president from 1856. His second term as president came after a coup d'état in 1871, during which he helped stabilize the nation's economy and governance. Roberts passed away on February 24, 1876, in Monrovia, Liberia, leaving behind a legacy of leadership, resilience, and vision that continues to inspire. His life's work significantly impacted the history of Liberia and the broader narrative of African-American repatriation and governance.

In Norfolk, Virginia, Joe Roberts was born,
With a spirit so strong, not to be torn.
He sailed to Liberia, seeking a new start,
And ended up leading with brains and heart.

As a merchant, he thrived, in Africa's land,
Then into politics, he made a grandstand.
Becoming president not once but twice,
His leadership was like sugar and spice.

From '48 to '56, he steered the ship,
Then returned again with a presidential grip.
His efforts were key to Liberia's flight,
Into independence, shining so bright.

But Joe wasn't just about politics and fame,
He helped Liberia's education claim.
As president, he didn't rest on his seat,
He aimed for progress, not just defeat.

Today, if Joe were still around,
He'd be found on his feet, not on the ground.
Advocating for justice, leading the way,
In building a better tomorrow, come what may.

For men today, a lesson to heed,
From Joe's life, we can surely feed.
With vision, resilience, and grace,
They can make their mark, in any place.

So let's raise a toast to Joe Roberts, dear,
A pioneer we hold so near.
His legacy lives on, forever proud,
In every black man, standing tall and unbowed.

Samora Machel of Mozambique

Samora Machel, a towering figure in Mozambican and African history, was born on September 29, 1933. He emerged as a prominent leader during Mozambique's struggle for independence from Portuguese colonial rule. Machel's journey into leadership began with his involvement in the Mozambican Liberation Front (FRELIMO), a liberation movement founded in 1962. He quickly rose through the ranks, becoming FRELIMO's military commander and leading the armed struggle against Portuguese colonial forces. Under Machel's leadership, FRELIMO waged a protracted guerrilla war that ultimately culminated in Mozambique's independence in 1975. Machel played a central role in negotiating Mozambique's transition to independence, and he became the country's first President upon its liberation from colonial rule.

As President, Machel embarked on a comprehensive program of nation-building and social transformation. He implemented agrarian reforms aimed at redistributing land to peasants, promoted education and healthcare initiatives, and prioritized infrastructure development to modernize the country. Machel's leadership extended beyond Mozambique's borders, as he emerged as a key figure in the struggle against apartheid in neighboring South Africa. He provided support to the African National Congress (ANC) and other liberation movements fighting against the oppressive apartheid regime. Tragically, Machel's life was cut short in 1986 when the plane he was traveling in crashed near the South African border under suspicious circumstances. Although his death remains shrouded in controversy, Machel's legacy as a champion of African liberation, social justice, and Pan-Africanism endures. Today, Machel is remembered as a symbol of Mozambique's struggle for independence and a beacon of hope for the African continent. His unwavering commitment to the principles of freedom, equality, and solidarity continues to inspire generations of Africans striving for a better future.

In Mozambique's tale, a hero stood tall,
Samora Machel, heeding freedom's call.
Born in September's gentle breeze,
A leader bold, with fire to seize.

FRELIMO's commander, in battle array,
Against Portuguese rule, he'd make his way.
Through guerrilla war, he'd lead the fight,
For Mozambique's dawn, in freedom's light.

Independence won, in '75's grace,
Machel's vision, a nation to embrace.
President he became, with a smile so bright,
A new era dawned, in Mozambique's sight.

Agrarian reforms, land to share,
Education and healthcare, for all to bear.
Infrastructure booming, modernization's plan,
Under Machel's rule, Mozambique ran.

But beyond the borders, his voice would chime,
In South Africa's struggle, against apartheid's crime.
Supporting the ANC, in their quest for right,
Machel stood firm, in freedom's fight.

Tragically, fate struck, in '86's tear,
A plane crash silenced, a leader so dear.
Yet Machel's legacy, in hearts does dwell,
A beacon of hope, in freedom's swell.

If Machel walked among us today,
In Pan-Africanism, he'd lead the way.
Advocating justice, with all his might,
In every action, in every fight.

Men of today, his spirit embrace,
In leadership, leave a lasting trace.
Emulate his passion, his fervent stride,
Make black men proud, with hearts open wide.

For Machel's legacy, forever true,
In freedom's quest, he leads anew.
A symbol of hope, in Africa's heart,
Samora Machel, shall never depart.

Amílcar Cabral of Guinea-Bissau and Cape Verde

Amílcar Cabral, a towering figure in the struggle for African liberation, was born on September 12, 1924, in Guinea-Bissau. He emerged as a prominent leader during the fight against Portuguese colonial rule in Guinea-Bissau and Cape Verde. Cabral's journey into leadership began with his involvement in the anti-colonial movement in the early 1950s. He co-founded the African Party for the Independence of Guinea and Cape Verde (PAIGC) in 1956, with the goal of achieving independence for both Guinea-Bissau and Cape Verde. Under Cabral's leadership, the PAIGC waged a protracted guerrilla war against Portuguese colonial forces. Cabral's strategic brilliance and unwavering determination played a crucial role in the success of the liberation struggle. He was instrumental in mobilizing support among rural populations and building a strong political and military infrastructure.

One of Cabral's most significant achievements was his development of the theory of "armed propaganda," which emphasized the importance of integrating political education with military action. This approach allowed the PAIGC to garner widespread support among the people and undermine the legitimacy of the colonial regime. In addition to his military leadership, Cabral was a visionary thinker and strategist. He articulated a clear vision for post-colonial Guinea-Bissau and Cape Verde, emphasizing the need for economic self-reliance, social justice, and Pan-African solidarity. Tragically, Cabral's life was cut short in 1973 when he was assassinated by members of his own party. Despite his untimely death, Cabral's legacy as a champion of African liberation and unity endures. His ideas continue to inspire liberation movements across the continent, and he is remembered as one of Africa's most visionary leaders.

In Guinea-Bissau's heart, a hero's tale,
Amílcar Cabral, heeding freedom's wail.
Born on September's breezy shore,
A leader bold, forevermore.

In the fight against colonial reign,
Cabral emerged, with courage untamed.
Co-founding PAIGC, the path he'd pave,
For Guinea-Bissau's and Cape Verde's brave.

Through guerrilla war, against the foe,
Cabral's brilliance, a radiant glow.
Mobilizing rural hearts, in unity's light,
With strategic might, he'd win the fight.

"Armed propaganda," his strategy bold,
Political education, in stories told.
With military might, and minds engaged,
Cabral's vision, forever staged.

Post-colonial dreams, he'd foresee,
Economic self-reliance, for all to see.
Social justice, Pan-African flame,
In Cabral's vision, Africa's name.

But fate dealt a blow, in '73's pain,
Assassinated, a loss so vain.
Yet Cabral's legacy, forever clear,
In African hearts, he's always near.

If Cabral walked among us today,
In Pan-Africanism, he'd lead the way.
Advocating justice, with all his might,
In every action, in every fight.

Men of today, his spirit embrace,
In leadership, leave a lasting trace.
Emulate his passion, his fervent stride,
Make black men proud, with hearts open wide.

For Cabral's legacy, a beacon's glow,
In freedom's quest, he'd lead the show.
A champion of liberation, forever in our heart,
Amílcar Cabral, shall never depart.

Kenneth Kaunda of Zambia

Kenneth Kaunda, a towering figure in Zambian and African history, was born on April 28, 1924. He emerged as a prominent leader during Zambia's struggle for independence from British colonial rule. Kaunda's journey into leadership began with his involvement in nationalist politics in the 1950s. He played a key role in the formation of the United National Independence Party (UNIP) in 1959, which became the leading political force in the fight against colonialism in Zambia. Under Kaunda's leadership, Zambia gained independence from British rule in 1964, and he became the country's first President. As President, Kaunda embarked on a mission to build a united, democratic, and prosperous Zambia. One of Kaunda's most significant achievements was his commitment to national unity and reconciliation. He implemented policies aimed at promoting ethnic harmony and bridging divisions between different groups within Zambian society.

Kaunda's vision of a "One Zambia, One Nation" ethos became a central tenet of Zambian identity and unity. Kaunda also prioritized economic development and social welfare. He implemented ambitious programs to modernize Zambia's infrastructure, promote industrialization, and expand access to education and healthcare. His efforts significantly improved living standards and opportunities for Zambians across the country. Internationally, Kaunda was a leading advocate for African liberation and solidarity. He provided support to liberation movements across the continent, including those in South Africa, Namibia, and Zimbabwe, in their struggles against colonialism and apartheid. Despite facing economic challenges and political opposition during his presidency, Kaunda remained committed to his principles of democracy, human rights, and social justice. He peacefully stepped down from power in 1991, setting a precedent for democratic transitions in Africa. Today, Kaunda is remembered as a statesman and a symbol of Zambian independence and unity. His legacy as a champion of African liberation and a visionary leader continues to inspire generations of Zambians and Africans alike.

In Zambia's tale, a leader bold,
Kenneth Kaunda, with stories untold.
Born on April's breezy morn,
A legacy, in history's adorn.

In nationalist fervor, he'd find his might,
With UNIP, he'd take flight.
Against colonial chains, he'd stand,
Leading Zambia to freedom's land.

As President, his vision clear,
Unity and prosperity, drawing near.
"One Zambia, One Nation," he'd decree,
A chorus of hope, for all to see.

Economic development, his fervent goal,
Modernization, for every soul.
Education and healthcare, he'd impart,
Kaunda's vision, a beating heart.

Internationally, his voice would ring,
In African unity, he'd sing.
Liberation movements, he'd aid,
In solidarity, his legacy laid.

Facing challenges, with courage untold,
Kaunda stood firm, in truth and bold.
Stepping down, with grace and might,
A beacon of democracy, shining bright.

If Kaunda walked among us today,
In leadership, he'd lead the way.
Embracing unity, with every stride,
Injustice, he'd never abide.

Men of today, his spirit embrace,
In humility, leave a lasting trace.
Emulate his principles, his stand,
Make black men proud, across the land.

For Kaunda's legacy, forever enshrined,
In Zambia's heart, his spirit aligned.
A champion of freedom, in every vow,
Kenneth Kaunda, our hero now.

Ellen Johnson Sirleaf of Liberia

Ellen Johnson Sirleaf, born on October 29, 1938, in Liberia, emerged as a transformative figure in African politics, becoming the first female President of Liberia and the first female head of state in Africa. Her journey into leadership began with a background in finance and economics, including roles at the World Bank and the United Nations Development Programme. Sirleaf's political career gained momentum in the 1980s, and she became known for her advocacy for democracy and good governance in Liberia. Despite facing imprisonment and exile during the regimes of Samuel Doe and Charles Taylor, Sirleaf remained committed to her vision of a democratic and prosperous Liberia. In 2005, Sirleaf made history by winning the presidential election in Liberia, marking the country's first peaceful transition of power in decades. As President, she focused on rebuilding Liberia's war-torn economy and infrastructure, promoting reconciliation and peace, and combating corruption.

Sirleaf's tenure as President was marked by significant achievements, including stabilizing Liberia's economy, attracting foreign investment, and improving access to education and healthcare. She also played a key role in securing debt relief for Liberia and fostering partnerships with international organizations and donor countries. Additionally, Sirleaf's leadership during the Ebola crisis in 2014 demonstrated her commitment to crisis management and public health. Under her guidance, Liberia successfully contained the outbreak and implemented measures to prevent future epidemics. In 2011, Sirleaf was awarded the Nobel Peace Prize for her efforts to promote peace and democracy in Liberia and her role as a champion for women's rights. Despite criticism and challenges during her presidency, Sirleaf's legacy as a trailblazer for women in African politics and a champion of democracy and development in Liberia endures.

In Liberia's tale, a woman bold,
Ellen Johnson Sirleaf, stories untold.
Born on October's vibrant hue,
A leader emerged, strong and true.

In finance and economics, she'd thrive,
At the World Bank, she'd strive.
Her journey to leadership, a steady climb,
In advocacy, for democracy's chime.

Imprisonment and exile, she'd face,
Yet, in her vision, she'd find grace.
For a democratic Liberia, she'd fight,
In darkness, she'd be the light.

In 2005, history she'd make,
The first female President, for goodness' sake!
Rebuilding Liberia's shattered dreams,
In her hands, hope gleams.

Stabilizing the economy, her aim,
Attracting investment, in her game.
Education and healthcare, she'd enhance,
In her leadership, a vibrant dance.

Debt relief, she'd secure,
Partnerships forged, strong and sure.
During Ebola's dark night,
Her leadership, a beacon bright.

Nobel Peace Prize, in her hand,
For peace and democracy, a stand.
Despite challenges, she'd endure,
Her legacy, forever pure.

As Sirleaf walks among us today,
In women's empowerment, she continues to lead
the way.
Embracing strength, with every stride,
In her footsteps, let us abide.

Women of today, her spirit embrace,
In leadership, leave a lasting trace.
Emulate her courage, her grace,
Make black women proud, in every space.

For Sirleaf's legacy, forever enshrined,
A beacon of hope, for womankind.
A trailblazer, in every vow,
Ellen Johnson Sirleaf, our hero now.

Nnamdi Azikiwe of Nigeria

Nnamdi Azikiwe often referred to as "Zik of Africa," was a Nigerian nationalist, statesman, and the first President of Nigeria (1963-1966). Born on November 16, 1904, in Zungeru, Nigeria, then a British protectorate, Azikiwe played a pivotal role in Nigeria's struggle for independence and its subsequent nation-building efforts. Azikiwe was a prominent figure in the Nigerian nationalist movement, advocating for Nigeria's independence from British colonial rule. He co-founded the National Council of Nigeria and the Cameroons (NCNC), a political party that championed the cause of Nigerian self-governance. Azikiwe was also a skilled journalist and editor. He founded and edited several newspapers, including the West African Pilot, which became a platform for his nationalist ideas. Through journalism, he propagated the message of self-rule and galvanized support for the independence movement. Azikiwe was also committed to education and played a key role in the establishment of various educational institutions in Nigeria.

Azikiwe served in various political capacities, including as Premier of the Eastern Region of Nigeria from 1954 to 1959. He was a key negotiator in the lead-up to Nigeria's independence in 1960, and subsequently served as the country's first Governor-General (1960-1963) and later as its first President (1963-1966) after Nigeria became a republic. He was a staunch advocate for Pan-Africanism, believing in the unity and solidarity of African nations. He played a significant role in the Pan-African movement, attending conferences and collaborating with other African leaders to promote African unity and decolonization. Azikiwe's legacy as a nationalist leader and statesman remains influential in Nigeria and across Africa. He is remembered for his contributions to Nigeria's independence struggle, his efforts in nation-building, and his advocacy for African unity. Numerous institutions, streets, and monuments across Nigeria bear his name in honor of his contributions to the country's history and development. Nnamdi Azikiwe passed away on May 11, 1996, but his legacy continues to inspire generations of Nigerians and Africans in their pursuit of freedom, unity, and progress.

In Zungeru, Nigeria, Zik was born,
A legend, a leader, from dusk until morn.
"Nnamdi Azikiwe," they called him with pride,
For Africa's future, he valiantly tried.

With wit and with wisdom, he took up the pen,
In newspapers bold, his voice echoed then.
As a journalist skilled, his words were a light,
Guiding his people through the colonial night.

In politics, too, Zik left his mark,
With passion and fervor, he embarked.
Premier, Governor-General, President esteemed,
In Nigeria's history, his legacy gleamed.

Pan-African dreams in his heart did reside,
In unity and strength, he found his stride.
From coast unto coast, his voice did resound,
In freedom and dignity, his dreams were found.

If Zik were alive in our world today,
He'd lead with conviction, in his own way.
Inspiring the youth, with tales of the past,
To build a bright future, where freedom will last.

So let's heed his call, let's take up the fight,
For justice, for freedom, in broad daylight.
With courage and honor, let's follow his lead,
And make black men proud, in word and in deed.

Félix Houphouët-Boigny of Côte d'Ivoire

Félix Houphouët-Boigny often referred to as the "Sage of Africa," was a towering figure in Ivorian and African politics. Born on October 18, 1905, in Yamoussoukro, Côte d'Ivoire, then a French colony, Houphouët-Boigny rose to prominence as a statesman and became the first President of Côte d'Ivoire, serving from 1960 until his death in 1993. Houphouët-Boigny played a crucial role in the struggle for Côte d'Ivoire's independence from French colonial rule. He skillfully navigated the political landscape, advocating for gradual self-governance rather than immediate independence, which earned him favor with French authorities while still advancing the cause of his people. As President,

Houphouët-Boigny emphasized national unity and stability, steering Côte d'Ivoire away from the ethnic and religious conflicts that plagued many African nations. He promoted a policy of "ivoirite," which aimed to create a strong national identity transcending ethnic divisions, and he actively encouraged economic development and modernization.

Under Houphouët-Boigny's leadership, Côte d'Ivoire experienced a period of economic prosperity, earning it the title of "The Jewel of West Africa." He implemented agricultural policies that transformed the country into the world's leading cocoa producer and diversified its economy through investments in infrastructure, education, and healthcare. Houphouët-Boigny was a prominent figure on the international stage, advocating for African interests and promoting peace and cooperation among nations. He played a key role in the formation of the Organization of African Unity (OAU) and was known for his mediation efforts in regional conflicts.

Even after his death, Houphouët-Boigny's legacy of peace and reconciliation endured in Côte d'Ivoire. His policy of national unity, coupled with his emphasis on dialogue and consensus-building, laid the foundation for peaceful transitions of power and contributed to the country's relative stability in the years following his presidency. Félix Houphouët-Boigny's vision and leadership continue to shape Côte d'Ivoire's trajectory and inspire leaders across Africa. He is remembered as a statesman who prioritized the well-being of his people, promoted unity and development, and left an indelible mark on Ivorian and African history.

In Yamoussoukro's breeze, a tale began,
Of Félix Houphouët-Boigny, a noble man.
The "Sage of Africa," wise and bright,
Guiding Côte d'Ivoire with all his might.

Born in colonial days, his path was clear,
To lead his people, without fear.
With wit and charm, he paved the way,
For independence, come what may.

In politics, he danced with grace,
Navigating with a smiling face.
A master of diplomacy, he'd jest and quip,
Earning favors with each diplomatic trip.

As President, his vision soared,
Unity and stability he adored.
"Ivoirite" he preached, with pride,
A nation united, side by side.

"The Jewel of West Africa," they'd say,
Under his leadership, each day.
Cocoa fields and schools did bloom,
In Houphouët-Boigny's Ivorian boom.

On the world stage, he'd take his stand,
For Africa's interests, he'd lend a hand.
Mediator, peacemaker, with grace,
Bringing nations together, in one embrace.

Though he's gone, his legacy shines bright,
A beacon of hope, in the darkest night.
Men of today, take heed and learn,
From Houphouët-Boigny's noble turn.

In unity and peace, let us strive,
To make black men proud, and truly thrive.
Emulate his vision, his heart so grand,
And build a future, hand in hand.

Yekuno Amlak, an influential figure in Ethiopian history

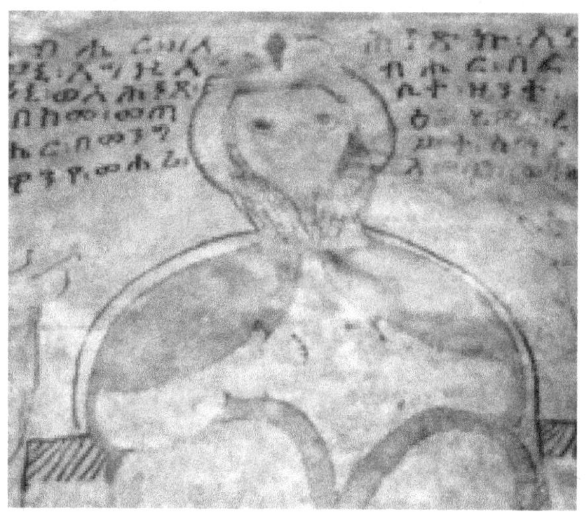

Yekuno Amlak is celebrated for restoring the Solomonic dynasty to the throne in 1270 after approximately 300 years of Zagwe dynasty rule. His reign, which lasted from 1270 to 1285, marked the beginning of a dynasty that would continue until 1974. Yekuno Amlak claimed descent from the biblical King Solomon, a lineage that was later enshrined in the Ethiopian constitution of 1955. He was a ruler from Bete Amhara, which is part of modern-day Wollo and northern Shewa, and he became Emperor of Ethiopia following the defeat of the last Zagwe king. This claim, however, is not supported by contemporary historical evidence but was a powerful narrative that legitimized his rule and the subsequent Solomonic dynasty. Educated at the Istifanos Monastery near Lake Hayq, Yekuno Amlak was said to have been raised and guided by Tekle Haymanot, who helped him overthrow the Zagwe king, although other accounts suggest it was Iyasus Mo'a, the abbot of Istifanos Monastery. The discrepancies in these accounts are attributed to the shifting prominence of religious institutions over time. Yekuno Amlak's reign is also noted for the construction of the Church of Gennete Maryam near Lalibela, which features some of the earliest surviving wall paintings in Ethiopia. His body was later re-interred in the church of Atronsa Maryam by his descendant, Emperor Baeda Maryam I.

Yekuno Amlak's ascension to power is often associated with a prophecy by a rooster, which foretold that whoever ate the rooster's head would become king. This story, while not contemporary with Yekuno Amlak, reflects the mystical aura that surrounded his rise to power. His reign saw the establishment of his capital in Tegulet in Shoa, continuing the southward movement of the Ethiopian state's center. During this period, Amharic began to replace Geez as the court language, although Geez remained the liturgical language of the Ethiopian Orthodox Church. The restoration of the Solomonic dynasty by Yekuno Amlak is a pivotal moment in Ethiopian history, as it not only reinstated a lineage that traced its roots back to ancient biblical times but also set the stage for the Church's increased wealth and power. This event also initiated what has been described as the era of "roving capitals," with the royal court frequently relocating throughout the kingdom. Yekuno Amlak's military campaigns against neighboring Islamic states marked the beginning of growing tensions that would shape the region's history for centuries. His legacy is a testament to the complex interplay of myth, religion, and power in the history of Ethiopia.

In the land of Ethiopia, ages past,
Lived Yekuno Amlak, whose shadow cast
A tale of grandeur, of wit, and might,
Restoring the throne, in Solomonic light.

From the mist of time, his legend springs,
As the rooster crowed, prophetic wings,
"Whoever dares to eat my head,
Shall reign supreme," the prophecy said.

With a chuckle, perhaps, or a bemused stare,
Yekuno Amlak pondered, without a care,
For a kingdom reclaimed, a dynasty restored,
He took a bite, and destiny soared.

Raised 'neath monastery's sacred dome,
Guided by Tekle Haymanot, to roam,
Or was it Iyasus Mo'a's hand,
That led him to power, across the land?

In Tegulet's halls, his court did thrive,
With Amharic tongues, they kept alive,
The legacy of kings of old,
In tales of glory, forever told.

Now, if Yekuno Amlak walked today's earth,
What might he do, for what it's worth?
With wisdom gleaned from times of yore,
He'd inspire change, forevermore.

A leader bold, with vision clear,
Guiding his people without fear,
Injustice he'd battle, with righteous might,
For every man, woman, child, in his sight.

To emulate him, men of today,
Should grasp his essence, come what may,
With resilience and honor, stand tall,
And let their actions speak, to all.

Proudly, they'd walk, in his noble stride,
With dignity and grace, as their guide,
For Yekuno Amlak, in history's light,
Shows us the way, to shine so bright.

So let us honor, this legend grand,
Whose reign reshaped, Ethiopian land,
And in his footsteps, let us trod,
For Yekuno Amlak, a beacon of God.

William Vacanarat Shadrach Tubman of Liberia

William Tubman, born on November 29, 1895, in Harper, Liberia, was a pivotal figure in Liberian history, serving as the country's 19th president from 1944 until his death in 1971. His presidency, which spanned 27 years, remains the longest in the nation's history, earning him the title of "father of modern Liberia" for his significant contributions to the country's modernization. Tubman's administration was marked by substantial foreign investment, which facilitated economic and infrastructural development, leading to a period of prosperity. He implemented the National

Unification Policy, aimed at reducing the disparities between Americo-Liberians and indigenous Liberians, fostering a more cohesive national identity. Tubman's early life was steeped in discipline and poverty, which shaped his character and future policies. His grandfather, a Methodist preacher and former Speaker of the Liberian House of Representatives, and his parents, who were descendants of freed American slaves, influenced his upbringing. Tubman's political journey began with his service as a junior customs collector, where he demonstrated competence and integrity. His legal acumen, honed through self-study, propelled him into public service, leading to various roles including trial judge, public prosecutor, and senator. His advocacy for the constitutional rights of the majority tribespeople and his strategic political maneuvers earned him the presidency. During his tenure, Tubman enacted reforms such as suffrage and property rights for women, direct government participation for tribespeople, and the establishment of a public school system. His legacy is a testament to his commitment to progress and unity in Liberia.

In Harper, Liberia, on a fine November day,
William Tubman entered the world in his own special
way.
With a name so grand, it's hard not to cheer,
For William Vacanarat Shadrach Tubman, our hero so
dear!

From humble beginnings, he rose to great heights,
A leader whose legacy shines through dark nights.
For 27 years, he guided Liberia's path,
Through prosperity and unity, he avoided wrath.

As the father of modern Liberia, he's known,
For his vision and deeds, his seeds he has sown.
Bringing investment and progress to his land,
Tubman's leadership was truly grand.

With a twinkle in his eye and a stride so bold,
He tackled disparities, making his people one fold.
The National Unification Policy was his quest,
To bring harmony and peace, he gave his best.

Born in discipline, shaped by poverty's hand,
He rose above, like a ship on command.
From junior collector to President so tall,
Tubman's journey inspires, one and all.

If Tubman were here, what would he do?
Perhaps advocate for justice, through and through.
Encouraging unity, breaking down walls,
Empowering all, as his legacy calls.

Men of today, take heed of his tale,
With integrity and courage, you will prevail.
Emulate Tubman, make your ancestors proud,
In your actions, let their voices be loud.

For Tubman's spirit lives on in every stride,
In every fight for justice, with honor as our guide.
So here's to William Vacanarat Shadrach Tubman, our
friend,
His legacy forever, to the very end!

Muhammad Idris bin Muhammad al-Mahdi as-Senussi of Libya

Muhammad al-Mahdi as-Senussi, known as King Idris of Libya, was a pivotal figure in the country's history. Born into the Senussi Order, a political-religious Sufi Muslim order, he ascended to leadership after his cousin's abdication. His reign as King of Libya began on December 24, 1951, marking the establishment of the United Kingdom of Libya, which later became the Kingdom of Libya. Prior to his kingship, he served as Emir of Cyrenaica and Tripolitania, regions he would later unify under the Libyan crown. Idris's leadership was instrumental in ending hostilities with the Italians through the Modus vivendi of Acroma, leading to the recognition of Senussi control over most of Cyrenaica. His strategic alliances with Western powers allowed for economic aid and the establishment of military bases in Libya, which were crucial during the Cold War era. The discovery of oil in 1959 under his rule transformed the Libyan economy, ushering in a period of rapid economic growth.

However, his tenure was also marked by political challenges. The prohibition of political parties and the establishment of a unitary state in 1963, replacing Libya's federal system, were controversial moves that fueled opposition. The rise of Arab nationalism and socialism, coupled with corruption and close ties with the West, eventually led to his overthrow in the 1969 coup d'état led by Muammar Gaddafi. Despite these challenges, Idris's legacy includes significant contributions to Libya's national development. He promoted programs for economic development and worked to create national institutions such as the army and parliament. His efforts in developing the Sanusi order into a politically active and ideologically conservative force shaped Libyan nationalism and had lasting impacts on the nation's identity.

In Libya's annals, a tale unfolds,
Of a king whose story still holds,
Muhammad Idris, Senussi's pride,
In history's pages, he did reside.

Born into faith, Sufi's embrace,
His journey led to a kingly place.
From Cyrenaica's Emir he arose,
To unify lands, his prowess shows.

On December's eve, in '51,
His reign began beneath the sun.
United Kingdom of Libya's crown,
In his hands, a nation found.

A diplomat, strategic and wise,
With Western allies, he did ally.
Economic booms, oil's gleam,
Under his rule, a nation's dream.

But challenges came, as they often do,
Political storms, he weathered through.
Unitary state, a controversial change,
Yet in his vision, Libya would rearrange.

In halls of power, he sought to build,
Institutions strong, his vision fulfilled.
Army, parliament, symbols of pride,
In Libya's heart, they did reside.

Today, if he were here anew,
Idris might steer a different view.
Guiding Libya through modern ways,
In a world reshaped by changing days.

Men of today, heed his call,
Emulate his virtues, stand tall.
In his footsteps, let us stride,
With wisdom, grace, and honor guide.

For black men proud, his legacy shines,
In history's tapestry, it defines.
A leader true, in times of yore,
Muhammad Idris, forevermore.

Muhammad VIII al-Amin of Tunisia

Muhammad VIII al-Amin, known as Lamine Bey, was the last Bey of Tunis from 1943 to 1956 and the only King of Tunisia from 1956 to 1957. His reign was marked by significant events and transitions. He ascended to the throne during World War II after the deposition of his predecessor by the French Resident General. Recognized for his legitimacy posthumously by the Tunisian people, he initially sought to align with the Tunisian national movement against French colonial rule. However, his acceptance of French-initiated reforms in 1954 led to his estrangement from the nationalist Neo Destour party. Despite this, his reign oversaw the pivotal transition from a French protectorate to an independent state. His term as king was short-lived; following Tunisia's independence, he was deposed, and his properties were seized. Muhammad VIII al-Amin spent his final years in a modest apartment in Tunis, reflecting a dramatic change from his earlier status as a monarch.

In Tunis' storied past, there reigned a king,
Whose tale of twists and turns still makes hearts sing.
Muhammad VIII al-Amin, Lamine Bey in the fray,
A ruler of wit and charm, in a tumultuous day.

From Bey to King, his journey was profound,
Amidst the shifting sands, he held his ground.
In wartime chaos, he took his royal seat,
Navigating treacherous waters, oh, what a feat!

French colonial rule, a formidable foe,
Yet Lamine Bey danced to his own tempo.
He stood with his people, seeking freedom's light,
But French reforms caused a nationalist plight.

With dignity and grace, he faced his fate,
As Tunisia charted its independent state.
From palace halls to a modest abode,
His story tells of humility's noble code.

If he were here today, what would he do?
Perhaps mentor leaders, both old and new.
His legacy shines, a beacon so bright,
In times of change, he's a guiding light.

Men of today, take heed and learn,
From Lamine Bey's wisdom, let it burn.
Embrace humility, stand tall and proud,
In unity and grace, let your voices loud.

For Muhammad VIII al-Amin, his tale does live,
In the hearts of those who dare to give.
To make black men proud, let his spirit soar,
For in his story, we find strength galore.

Mohammed al-Khamis bin Yusef bin Hassan al-Alawi of Morocco

Mohammed al-Khamis bin Yusef bin Hassan al-Alawi, better known as Mohammed V, was born on August 10, 1909, and was a pivotal figure in Morocco's history, serving as the last Sultan from 1927 to 1953 and from 1955 to 1957, and as the first King from 1957 until his death in 1961. His reign was marked by the struggle for Moroccan independence from French and Spanish colonial rule. Early in his rule, he faced backlash for approving the Berber Dahir, which spurred Moroccan nationalism and opposition to French rule. Over time,

Mohammed V's support for the nationalist movement grew, and during World War II, he aligned with the Allies and took steps to protect Moroccan Jews from persecution. His historic speech in Tangier in 1947 openly called for independence and emphasized Morocco's Arab ties, further straining relations with France. The French authorities deposed and exiled him in 1953, but his absence only fueled the independence movement. Mohammed V's return to Morocco in 1955 was a turning point, leading to the country's independence in 1956. As King, he worked to consolidate national unity and modernize the country. His legacy is celebrated in Morocco, where he is remembered as a symbol of resistance and a father of the nation.

In Morocco's tale of yesteryears,
There lived a king, banishing fears.
Mohammed V, with regal flair,
Led his people with utmost care.

From Sultan to King, his journey grand,
He shaped Morocco's sovereign stand.
Born in August's warm embrace,
A leader with courage, wit, and grace.

Against colonial rule, he fought,
With every ounce of strength he brought.
The Berber Dahir, a bold decree,
Stirred the flames of liberty.

In World War's tumult, he took a stand,
Shielding Moroccan Jews, hand in hand.
His words in Tangier, ringing true,
Called for freedom, skies anew.

Exiled and deposed, he stood tall,
His absence only fueling the call.
Return he did, to jubilant cries,
Independence lighting up the skies.

Now, if he walked among us here,
His legacy bright, crystal clear.
Guiding men with wisdom's light,
Through darkened paths, to freedom's height.

In today's world, his spirit lives,
In every heart that courage gives.
Men of every hue and creed,
Embrace his values, take the lead.

To stand for justice, never yield,
And sow the seeds of unity's field.
In Mohammed V's footsteps tread,
To honor him, our souls we wed.

So let us learn from his grand tale,
And in his path, may we prevail.
For in our actions, let it be known,
The seeds of greatness, brightly sown.

Mohammed V, a beacon true,
A man of honor, through and through.
In every man, his spirit blooms,
Guiding us to brighter tomorrow's rooms.

Ahmadou Babatoura Ahidjo of Cameroon

Ahmadou Ahidjo was a pivotal figure in Cameroon's history, serving as the country's first president from 1960 until his resignation in 1982. Born on August 24, 1924, in Garoua, Cameroon, Ahidjo played a significant role in the nation's independence from France and worked towards the unification of the French and English-speaking regions of the country. His tenure saw the establishment of a centralized political system and the creation of a single-party state under the Cameroon National Union in 1966. In 1972, he abolished the federation in favor of a unitary state, further solidifying his vision of a unified Cameroon. Despite his controversial resignation and subsequent life in exile, Ahidjo's early efforts in building a stable and prosperous nation are remembered as a cornerstone of Cameroon's development.

In Garoua's heart, a leader was born,
Ahmadou Ahidjo, history's adorn.
From Cameroon's cradle, he arose,
To shape its destiny, no one opposes.

In '60, he took the presidential helm,
Guiding his nation, his steady realm.
French shackles loosened, independence gleamed,
In his vision, a united dream.

With wit and charm, he bridged divides,
French, English, together he guides.
Centralized power, a single-party state,
Ahidjo's Cameroon, a decisive fate.

In '72, federations fell,
Unitary state, Ahidjo's spell.
Bold decisions, some may debate,
Yet unity prevailed, in his state.

Now if he wandered this earthly sphere,
Ahidjo's wisdom would surely steer.
Perhaps he'd mentor, with a gentle hand,
Guiding leaders to understand.

Men of today, in his steps tread,
Building bridges, not walls, instead.
His legacy echoes, loud and clear,
In Cameroon's heart, he's ever near.

So let's raise a toast to Ahmadou's name,
A leader, a legend, in history's frame.
His spirit lives on, let it be avowed,
Making black men proud, standing tall and proud.

Sylvanus Épiphanio Olympio of Togo

Sylvanus Épiphanio Olympio was a significant political figure in Togo. He served as the first Prime Minister and then the first President of Togo after the country's independence. Born on September 6, 1902, in Kpandu, Togoland, Olympio was part of the influential Olympio family. His education at the London School of Economics prepared him for a successful career at Unilever, where he eventually became the general manager for Africa. His political career began to take shape post-World War II when he became a leading figure in Togo's movement for independence. His party won the 1958 election, and he became Prime Minister, leading Togo to complete independence in 1960. As President, Olympio worked towards the unification of the Ewe people and sought to reduce French influence in the region. Unfortunately, his presidency was cut short when he was assassinated during a military coup in 1963. His legacy includes his efforts to establish a stable and independent Togolese state and his vision for a united Africa.

In Togo's tale of yore, a man of grace,
Sylvanus Olympio, with a determined face.
From Kpandu's embrace, he rose to lead,
A nation's destiny, with valor indeed.

Born into the Olympio fold, he came,
With London's teachings, he staked his claim.
Unilever's helm, he did ably steer,
Across Africa's lands, without a fear.

Post-war whispers birthed his political fire,
Independence calls, his heart did inspire.
With eloquence and wit, he led the fight,
For Togo's freedom, day and night.

In '58, victory's sweet song did chime,
Prime Minister he became, in his prime.
With fervor unbound, he charted the course,
To sovereignty's shores, without remorse.

As President, his vision did gleam,
Unity for Ewe, like a cherished dream.
French influence waned, as he dared to tread,
Towards a Togo, by Togolese led.

But alas, fate's cruel twist did unfold,
In '63, tragedy's tale was told.
A coup's cold hand snatched him away,
Leaving Togo mourning, in dismay.

Yet, Olympio's legacy shines bright,
A beacon of hope in freedom's light.
For in his footsteps, men today should tread,
With courage and honor, in heart and head.

If he walked amongst us, what would he do?
Guide Africa's sons to vistas anew.
With wisdom and grace, he'd lead the way,
Towards a brighter, unified day.

So let us emulate, his courage and might,
Stand tall and proud, in truth's pure light.
For Sylvanus Olympio, a hero true,
Shows us what black men can achieve and do.

Philibert Tsiranana of Madagascar

Philibert Tsiranana, born on October 18, 1912, in Ambarikorano, Madagascar, was a pivotal figure in Malagasy history, serving as the first President of Madagascar from 1959 to 1972. His tenure as president was marked by a period of stability and moderate economic growth, earning Madagascar the moniker "the Happy Island." Tsiranana's policies were rooted in social democracy, and under his leadership, Madagascar maintained close ties with France and other Western nations, even after gaining independence. A former professor of French and mathematics, Tsiranana's rise to power began with his election as a deputy in the French National Assembly in

1956, followed by his founding of the Social Democratic Party of Madagascar. He played a crucial role in Madagascar's peaceful transition to independence, which was proclaimed on June 26, 1960. Despite his popularity and initial success, his presidency faced challenges, including accusations of authoritarian tendencies and electoral issues. His administration came to an end following widespread protests, leading to the establishment of the Second Republic. Tsiranana's legacy is complex; while he is remembered as the "Father of Independence," his later years in power were marred by political unrest and opposition to his policies.

In Ambarikorano, the tale began,
With Philibert Tsiranana, a remarkable man.
Born on October's fine and golden scene,
To shape the destiny of Madagascar, serene.

A scholar of numbers, a master of words,
In French and in math, his intellect soared.
But destiny called him to a higher stage,
To lead his people, on history's page.

From the classrooms to the political floor,
He rose with a vision, to open new doors.
With charm and wit, and a smile so bright,
He guided Madagascar into the light.

As the first President, his reign did start,
A period of peace, a hopeful heart.
"The Happy Island," they fondly said,
Under his rule, joy blossomed and spread.

Social democracy, his guiding creed,
Building bridges where others would impede.
With France and the West, he kept ties strong,
In unity and progress, he found where he belonged.

Independence came, a historic day,
With Tsiranana leading the Malagasy way.
June 26th, 1960, a nation's pride unfurled,
In peaceful transition, freedom's flag swirled.

Yet challenges came, as they often do,
Accusations flew, and unrest grew.
Authoritarian whispers, electoral strife,
Testing the fabric of Madagascar's life.

But let's not forget his legacy true,
A man who dared what few could pursue.
In today's world, his example stands tall,
To lead with grace, to rise after a fall.

If Philibert walked among us now,
Perhaps he'd advocate, with furrowed brow.
For unity, for peace, for progress to see,
That all men, black or white, can truly be free.

So let us, men of today, take heed,
In Tsiranana's footsteps, plant our seed.
To lead with honor, to strive for the right,
And make our brothers proud, in day and night.

Samuel Shafiishuna Daniel Nujoma of Namibia

Sam Nujoma, born on May 12, 1929, is a prominent Namibian revolutionary, anti-apartheid activist, and politician renowned for his pivotal role in the fight for Namibia's independence. As a founding member and the first president of the South West Africa People's Organization (SWAPO), Nujoma was instrumental in leading the national liberation movement against South African rule. His leadership extended to the establishment of the People's Liberation Army of Namibia (PLAN), launching a guerrilla war against the apartheid government of South Africa in 1966. This marked the beginning of the Namibian War of Independence, which lasted until 1989. Nujoma's political career is marked by his three-term presidency of Namibia, from 1990 to 2005, during which he oversaw the country's transition from South African occupation to sovereignty.

Nujoma's early life in Ongandjera, Ovamboland, was characterized by his involvement in anti-colonial politics, which intensified after the Old Location resistance in 1958. His subsequent arrest and deportation did not deter his commitment to Namibia's liberation. In 1960, he sought exile in Tanzania, receiving support from Julius Nyerere, which further solidified his resolve to fight for independence. Throughout his career, Nujoma has been honored with numerous awards, including the Lenin Peace Prize, the Indira Gandhi Peace Prize, and the Ho Chi Minh Peace Prize, recognizing his contributions to peace and independence.

His autobiography, "Where Others Wavered," published in 2005, provides a personal account of his journey and the challenges faced during the liberation struggle. The Parliament of Namibia has bestowed upon him the titles "Founding President of the Republic of Namibia" and "Father of the Namibian Nation," acknowledging his foundational role in the nation's history. Nujoma's legacy continues to influence Namibian politics and society, and his life's work remains a testament to the power of resilience and leadership in the face of adversity.

In the heart of Africa's gleaming sands,
Stood a man with revolutionary hands.
Samuel Shafiishuna Daniel Nujoma, they say,
Led Namibia's charge, come what may.

Born in '29, on May's twelfth day,
He'd lead a nation's fervent sway.
A stalwart fighter, against apartheid's might,
His courage sparked the darkest night.

In Ovamboland's embrace, he found his voice,
Defying chains, he made the bold choice.
To Tanzania's shores, he sought his flight,
With Nyerere's embrace, he'd take his fight.

From the trenches of struggle, he rose high,
As SWAPO's leader, reaching for the sky.
With PLAN's guerrilla warriors, he'd stand tall,
Fighting oppression's damning call.

Three terms as president, a nation's guide,
Through trials and triumphs, he'd stride.
Transitioning from chains to sovereign might,
His vision fueled Namibia's flight.

The Lenin Peace Prize adorned his chest,
With Indira Gandhi's laurels, he'd rest.
Ho Chi Minh's nod, a testament grand,
To Nujoma's resolve, across the land.

Now if he roamed in today's bright dawn,
His wisdom and grit would linger on.
Leading with grace, in a world of strife,
Urging unity to shape a brighter life.

Men of today, take heed and learn,
From Nujoma's fire, let it burn.
Embrace resilience, in the face of fear,
Forge paths of progress, far and near.

Let his legacy echo, loud and clear,
Men of today, hold it dear.
For in his courage, we find our way,
Making black men proud, every day.

António Agostinho Neto of Angola

Agostinho Neto, born on September 17, 1922, in Icolo e Bengo, Angola, was a man of many facets: a revolutionary leader, a dedicated physician, and a gifted poet. His journey from a medical student to the first president of Angola is a testament to his unwavering commitment to his country's liberation from colonial rule. Neto's political activism began during his university years in Portugal, where he was arrested multiple times for his involvement in the anti-colonial movement. Despite these setbacks, he completed his medical studies and returned to Angola, only to be arrested again for his continued opposition to colonial authorities. His escape to Morocco marked the beginning of his formal engagement with the Angolan liberation movement, leading to his election as president of the Popular Movement for the Liberation of Angola (MPLA) in 1962.

Neto's leadership was pivotal in Angola's struggle for independence, which was achieved in 1975. As the nation's first president, he faced the immense challenge of uniting a country divided by civil war. His administration focused on social and economic reforms, aiming to improve education, healthcare, and infrastructure. Under his presidency, Angola made significant strides in gaining international recognition and support, despite the ongoing conflict with rival independence movements. Neto's tenure as president, though cut short by his untimely death in 1979, left an indelible mark on Angola's history.

In addition to his political achievements, Neto was also celebrated for his literary contributions. His poetry, characterized by themes of cultural identity, resistance, and hope, resonated with the Angolan people's aspirations for freedom and dignity. His works were published in various Portuguese and Angolan reviews and anthologies, reflecting the depth of his intellectual and artistic vision. Today, Neto's legacy lives on, not only through the institutions he helped establish but also through the enduring power of his words, which continue to inspire future generations. His birthday is commemorated as National Heroes' Day, a public holiday that honors his contributions to Angola's independence and national identity. Neto's life and work remain a beacon of courage and resilience, embodying the spirit of a nation's quest for self-determination and progress.

In Icolo e Bengo, where the sun shines bright,
Lived a man who fought with all his might.
Born on September's seventeenth day,
Neto's legacy still lights our way.

A doctor turned leader, a poet at heart,
He played many roles, each a crucial part.
With pen and with scalpel, he wielded his might,
In the struggle for freedom, he fought the good fight.

From Portugal's halls to Angola's soil,
He faced down oppression, turmoil, and toil.
Arrested, imprisoned, yet never dismayed,
For his people's liberation, he steadfastly stayed.

In the midst of the struggle, his words took flight,
Poems of resistance, of hope, and of light.
Through verses he penned, he inspired the land,
A beacon of courage, a hero so grand.

As Angola's first president, he led with grace,
Guiding the nation to a brighter place.
Education, healthcare, and progress he sought,
His vision for Angola, tirelessly fought.

If Neto walked among us in this day and age,
He'd advocate justice, on history's stage.
He'd champion the rights of the oppressed,
And strive for equality, nothing less.

Today's men should look to his example so true,
And strive to make black men proud in all they do.
With courage and resilience, let their voices resound,
For the fight for justice knows no bounds.

So let us honor Neto, on this special day,
His spirit lives on, in each courageous display.
For his legacy teaches us, in deeds and in song,
That the struggle for freedom must always be strong.

Sir Seewoosagur Ramgoolam of Mauritius

Sir Seewoosagur Ramgoolam, often referred to as SSR, was a pivotal figure in Mauritian history, revered as the father of the nation. Born on September 18, 1900, in Belle Rive, Mauritius, he rose from humble beginnings to become the first Prime Minister of independent Mauritius, serving from 1968 to 1982. His early life was marked by adversity, including the loss of his father at a young age and an accident that cost him his left eye. Despite these challenges, he pursued education with determination, eventually traveling to London to study medicine at University College and attending lectures at the London School of Economics. During his time in London, Ramgoolam was deeply influenced by the Indian independence movement and figures such as Mahatma Gandhi and Jawaharlal Nehru. He returned to Mauritius with a vision for social and political reform, which he began to implement as a leader of the Mauritius Labour Party. His efforts culminated in the historic achievement of Mauritian independence on March 12, 1968. As Prime Minister, Ramgoolam worked tirelessly to build the newly independent nation, instituting free universal education, establishing several hospitals, and organizing a comprehensive health care service.

He also played a significant role in local governance, serving as the Lord Mayor of Port Louis and later as the Chief Minister of Mauritius. His tenure saw the introduction of social security and pension systems, expansion of housing, and the lowering of the voting age to 18. His contributions to democracy and economic growth were recognized internationally, earning him a knighthood from Queen Elizabeth II in 1965 and the United Nations Prize for outstanding achievements in the field of human rights in 1973. After his tenure as Prime Minister, he served as the fifth Governor-General of Mauritius from 1983 until his death in 1985. His legacy continues to be honored throughout Mauritius, with the international airport, a national hospital, a medical college, and a botanical garden all bearing his name, a testament to his enduring impact on the nation he helped forge.

In Belle Rive, a legend took his first breath,
Sir Seewoosagur Ramgoolam, a name to bequeath.
With wit and charm, he danced through strife,
Crafting Mauritius' destiny with each stride of life.

Born to a land where dreams met the sea,
He soared beyond limits, breaking chains with glee.
An eye lost, but vision undimmed in his sight,
He marched on, fueled by justice's light.

From London's halls of learning, he drew inspiration,
Gandhi's resolve and Nehru's dedication.
Returning home, a leader he became,
A nation's father, igniting a flame.

Marching alongside history, hand in hand,
He birthed independence, a joyous band.
In governance, he toiled, a servant true,
Bringing hope to the many, not just the few.

Oh, imagine him now, in this modern age,
A beacon of wisdom on history's stage.
Perhaps he'd tweet with wit and grace,
Guiding nations with a digital embrace.

Men of today, take heed and learn,
From SSR's legacy, let it burn.
Embrace education, fight for what's right,
And in your deeds, let justice take flight.

For in every land, in every hue,
His spirit lives on, bold and true.
So let's make him proud, every single day,
And honor his memory in every way.

Sir Seretse Goitsebeng Maphiri Khama of Botswana

Sir Seretse Khama, born on July 1, 1921, in Serowe, Bechuanaland Protectorate, was a paramount figure in Botswana's transition from a British Protectorate to an independent nation. As the first President of Botswana, serving from 1966 until his death in 1980, Khama's leadership was pivotal in establishing the country's democratic and economic foundations. His presidency is noted for significant social and economic progress, including the establishment of a stable government, the promotion of education, and the development of natural resources which led to Botswana becoming one of the fastest-growing economies in the world. Khama's early life was marked by his royal lineage, being the grandson of King Khama III and the son of Sekgoma Khama II. After his father's untimely death, he ascended to the throne at the tender age of four, with his uncle Tshekedi Khama serving as regent. His education spanned several continents, beginning in South Africa at Fort Hare College and continuing in the United Kingdom at Balliol College, Oxford, and the Inner Temple in London, where he studied law.

His personal life also made international headlines due to his marriage to Ruth Williams, an Englishwoman, in 1948. This interracial union faced considerable opposition from the apartheid regime of South Africa and even caused diplomatic rifts, leading to Khama's exile from Bechuanaland. However, his unwavering commitment to his wife and his country eventually saw their return and his rise in politics. Khama co-founded the Botswana Democratic Party in 1962, which played a crucial role in advocating for independence. His tenure as Prime Minister began in 1965, and following independence in 1966, he was elected as the first President of Botswana. His administration was characterized by prudent economic policies, anti-corruption measures, and significant investments in infrastructure and public services.

Under Khama's leadership, Botswana established a reputation for stable governance and economic prudence, attracting foreign investment, particularly in the mining sector. His policies ensured that the wealth generated from diamond mining was reinvested into the nation, funding education, health, and infrastructure. Khama's vision extended beyond economic development; he was a proponent of social justice and worked towards reducing inequalities within his country. Khama's legacy is multifaceted; he is remembered as a statesman, a unifier, and a visionary leader who laid the groundwork for Botswana's future prosperity. His notable quote, "I think that the trouble we now face in the world is caused mainly by the refusal to try and see another man's point of view, to try and persuade by example — and the refusal to meet a rather passionate desire to impose your own will upon others, either by force or other means," reflects his philosophy of leadership and diplomacy. His death on July 13, 1980, marked the end of an era, but his impact on Botswana's political and economic landscape endures. Khama's son, Ian Khama, continued his legacy by serving as Botswana's fourth president from 2008 to

2018. Sir Seretse Khama's life and achievements remain a testament to his dedication to his country and his vision for a peaceful, prosperous, and equitable Botswana.

In Serowe, a tale began to bloom,
Of a man named Khama, whose destiny loomed.
Born into royalty, with a regal flair,
Sir Seretse Khama, beyond compare!

From childhood's throne, he rose so young,
With wisdom and grace, his heart was strung.
His quest for knowledge took him wide,
To Oxford's halls, he did confide.

With Ruth by his side, a love profound,
Their bond, a beacon, the world around.
Though strife and scorn did meet their way,
Their love prevailed, come what may!

In politics' fray, he took his stand,
A pioneer in a turbulent land.
Botswana's helm, he firmly gripped,
With policies sound, corruption he nipped!

Oh, Sir Seretse, with vision bright,
You paved the path, in darkest night.
From mining's wealth, you built anew,
Schools, hospitals, opportunities grew.

Your legacy vast, a shining light,
For leaders today, a guiding sight.
To seek understanding, to bridge the divide,
And in unity's embrace, let peace reside.

Men of today, take heed and learn,
From Khama's wisdom, let it burn.
To uplift, to empower, to make proud,
The legacy of greatness, shout it loud!

If Khama walked among us still,
His voice of reason, a mighty quill.
For justice, for progress, he'd strive,
In every heart, his spirit alive!

So let us emulate, let us aspire,
To kindle the flame, to reach higher.
For in Sir Seretse's footsteps, we find,
The power to unite, the strength of mankind.

Hastings Kamuzu Banda of Malawi

Hastings Kamuzu Banda, born circa 1898 near Kasungu, Malawi, was a significant figure in African politics, serving as the first president of Malawi from 1966 to 1994. His journey from a subsistence farmer's son to a leading nationalist is a testament to his determination and intellect. After pursuing education in the United States and obtaining a medical degree, he continued his studies in the United Kingdom to practice medicine within the British Empire. Banda's political involvement began in response to the proposed federation of Rhodesia and Nyasaland by white settlers, which he opposed due to the extension of white dominance it represented. His return to Nyasaland in 1958 was met with great enthusiasm, and he quickly became the president of the Nyasaland African Congress. Despite his initial imprisonment by colonial authorities, he played a pivotal role in achieving a majority for Africans in the Legislative Council and led his party to victory in the 1961 general elections. As prime minister, he guided Nyasaland to independence in 1964, subsequently becoming the first president when the nation was declared a republic in 1966. Banda's rule was marked by a mix of conservative economic policies and totalitarian political controls. He declared Malawi a one-party state under the Malawi Congress Party and later became President for Life. His tenure saw improvements in infrastructure and education relative to other African countries, and he was known for his anti-communist stance during the Cold War, which garnered Western support. However, his regime was also characterized by severe repression, with human rights groups estimating thousands of political opponents were killed, tortured, or jailed without trial. In the face of growing domestic and international pressure, Banda agreed to a referendum in 1993 that ended the one-party system. Although he ran for president in the subsequent democratic elections, he was defeated, marking the end of his three-decade rule.

In the heart of Africa's sun-kissed land,
Lived a man with a vision grand.
Hastings Kamuzu Banda was his name,
From humble roots, he rose to fame.

Born near Kasungu, a farmer's son,
His journey, oh, it had just begun.
A scholar, a healer, a leader bold,
His story, in history, firmly told.

From Malawi's fields to far-off shores,
He sought knowledge, he opened doors.
In the U.S. and U.K., he did strive,
To shape his nation, to make it thrive.

Opposing oppression, he took a stand,
Against colonial rule, he raised his hand.
With intellect sharp and willpower strong,
He fought for rights, against all wrongs.

President, Prime Minister, leader true,
His legacy, forever in view.
Yet, with humor and charm, he'd often jest,
A twinkle in his eye, never second best.

Now, if Banda were here today,
What would he do, what would he say?
Perhaps he'd advocate for unity,
And champion justice, with all his ingenuity.

Men of today, take heed and learn,
From Banda's courage, let it burn.
To stand for what's right, to break down walls,
And proudly heed your nation's calls.

Let his story inspire, let it ignite,
A flame within, shining bright.
For in emulating Banda's grace,
We honor his legacy, we proudly embrace.

So let us strive, let us aspire,
To make our world a bit brighter.
For in unity and progress, we find,
The essence of Banda's noble kind.

Ismail al-Azhari of Sudan

Ismail al-Azhari was a prominent Sudanese statesman who played a pivotal role in Sudan's transition to independence. Born on October 30, 1900, in Omdurman, Sudan, al-Azhari was educated at Gordon Memorial College in Khartoum and the American University of Beirut. His early career was marked by his presidency of the Graduates' General Congress in 1938, which advocated for Sudanese participation in the colonial administration. In 1943, he co-founded the Ashiggā' ("Brothers") party, which was the first political party in Sudan, and became a significant figure in the country's nationalist movement. Al-Azhari's political journey was characterized by his initial support for Sudan's union with Egypt, a stance that led to his arrest in 1948. However, as the first Sudanese prime minister after the 1953 elections, he shifted his position to advocate for complete independence in response to internal opposition and the risk of civil war. This pivotal decision facilitated Sudan's independence on January 1, 1956. Despite his early departure from office due to internal party rivalries, al-Azhari's influence on Sudanese politics remained significant. He returned to power in 1965 as the president of the Supreme Council, serving as the head of state until he was overthrown by a military coup in 1969. Ismail al-Azhari's legacy is marked by his leadership during a critical period of Sudanese history, his efforts towards educational and social reforms, and his ultimate realization of the importance of an independent Sudanese state.

In Omdurman town, where the Nile flows free,
Lived Ismail al-Azhari, a man of glee.
From Gordon College to Beirut's embrace,
His journey began with scholarly grace.

With passion aflame for Sudan's plight,
He stepped into politics, ready to fight.
In '38, he led the Congress of Grads,
Demanding rights, breaking colonial fads.

Co-founding Ashiggā', he blazed a trail,
For Sudan's future, he dared to prevail.
Union with Egypt, his first decree,
But independence called, loud as the sea.

Arrested in '48 for his fervent stance,
Yet undeterred, he continued his dance.
As prime minister, his vision was clear,
Complete freedom for Sudan, far and near.

January 1, '56, the day they'd yearned,
Independence dawned, the tables turned.
Though party squabbles cut his reign short,
His legacy shines, a bright, enduring fort.

Now, if al-Azhari walked among us today,
He'd champion rights in every way.
In education and social reform's glow,
He'd guide Sudan's path, helping it grow.

For men of today, his tale's profound,
To stand for justice, on solid ground.
To emulate his courage, his pride, his grace,
And make black men proud, in every place.

So let's raise a cheer, for Ismail al-Azhari,
A beacon of hope, in a world sometimes starry.
In history's book, his name's brightly lit,
A Sudanese hero, who'll never quit.

King Piankhi of Nubia

King Piankhi, also known as Piye, was a ruler of the ancient kingdom of Kush, located in what is now northern Sudan. He reigned from approximately 741 to 712 B.C. and is renowned for his conquest of Lower Egypt, which led to the establishment of the Twenty-fifth Dynasty, also referred to as the "Ethiopian Dynasty" of pharaohs. His reign marked one of the rare instances in African history where a power from the continent's interior significantly influenced Mediterranean politics. Piankhi's military campaigns were meticulously planned and executed, allowing him to take control of towns along the Nile one by one. His conquest culminated with the capture of Heliopolis in the Nile Delta, after which he considered Egypt under his domain and returned to his capital in Napata. Despite his departure, Piankhi left the Egyptian rulers in a tributary state, showcasing his strategic prowess and diplomatic acumen. Piankhi's legacy extends beyond his military achievements. He was a culturally conservative leader who sought to revive and strengthen traditional Egyptian institutions that were in decline. He oversaw the restoration of dilapidated temples during his brief stay in Lower Egypt and introduced the Egyptian custom of building pyramids for royal burials upon his return to Kush. A great pyramid was constructed for himself at Kuru, south of Napata, signifying his status and the cultural exchange between Egypt and Kush. Additionally, Piankhi was responsible for the construction of the temple at Jebel Barkal and several other temples in the Egyptian style, further cementing his role as a restorer of cultural heritage.

Piankhi's devotion to the god Amun was profound, and he commissioned significant renovations to the Great Temple of Amun at Jebel Barkal, a site of great religious importance. His stele at Amon, which details his military campaigns, is considered an invaluable historical document, providing insights into his reign and the period's events. Interestingly, Piankhi also had a noted affinity for horses, instituting the practice of adorning chariot teams and being remembered for this passion in various historical accounts. In summary, King Piankhi's achievements were multifaceted, encompassing military, cultural, and religious aspects. His successful campaigns against Egypt and subsequent rule over the region represented a significant shift in power dynamics, while his contributions to cultural and religious practices highlighted his commitment to preserving and revitalizing traditions. Piankhi's reign is a testament to the influence and capabilities of the Nubian kingdom during a pivotal time in African and Mediterranean history.

In ancient sands where Nile's waters flow,
Lived a king whose tales still glow.
Piankhi, they called him, with regal stride,
In Kush's embrace, he ruled with pride.

From dusty plains to Egypt's crown,
His armies marched, never backing down.
One by one, towns fell to his hand,
In Lower Egypt's grip, he made his stand.

Heliopolis, with its tales so old,
His conquest there, a story told.
Yet, with a wink and a nod, he knew,
Diplomacy's art, he mastered too.

Back to Napata, he turned his steed,
But Egypt's rulers, they still did heed.
For tribute flowed to Kush's throne,
A legacy grand, his name now known.

In temples vast, his faith he'd show,
To Amun, his reverence did grow.
Pyramids rose, touching the sky,
As cultural exchange soared high.

Jebel Barkal's temple, a marvel to see,
Piankhi's devotion, for all to agree.
Renovations grand, to Amun's delight,
In history's tapestry, he shines bright.

But let's imagine, if he were here,
In modern times, without a fear.
A leader still, with wisdom vast,
Guiding his people, ensuring they last.

In boardrooms filled with suits so fine,
Piankhi's voice would surely shine.
For strategy and vision, he'd be renowned,
In every endeavor, success would be found.

And in the hearts of men, his legacy lives,
A beacon of hope, a light that gives.
To emulate his strength, his grace,
Is to honor his memory, embrace his pace.

For men of today, in every hue,
Can learn from Piankhi, bold and true.
To lead with honor, to stand tall,
And make their ancestors proud, one and all.

So let's raise a toast to King Piankhi's name,
In history's annals, forever aflame.
For he showed the world what black men can do,
In ancient times and today, through and through.

King Sonni Ali of Songhai

King Sonni Ali, also known as Sonni Ali Ber, was a transformative figure in West African history, reigning from approximately 1464 to 1492 as the 15th ruler of the Songhai Empire. His leadership marked the beginning of the empire's expansion, turning a relatively small state along the Niger River into one of the most formidable empires in medieval Africa. Sonni Ali is celebrated for his military prowess and strategic acumen, which enabled him to conquer key trading cities such as Timbuktu and Djenne, thereby laying the foundation for Songhai's future prosperity and territorial dominance. His reign began with the conquest of Timbuktu in 1468, where he assisted the city's leaders in overthrowing the Tuareg occupiers. However, his methods were harsh, and he plundered the city, executing many of its inhabitants, which established his reputation as a ruthless leader. Despite this, his military campaigns were largely successful, and he expanded Songhai's territory significantly. He is particularly noted for his use of cavalry and riverine forces, which allowed him to control and protect the trade routes that were vital to the empire's economy.

Sonni Ali's approach to Islam was considered unorthodox by the Muslim scholars of his time. He practiced a blend of Islam with traditional Songhai religious customs, which did not endear him to the Islamic elite. Nevertheless, his ability to maintain and expand the empire's power was undeniable. His siege and eventual conquest of Jenne after a seven-year campaign further solidified his status as a formidable military leader. After repelling attacks from various groups, including the Mossi, the Fulani of the Dendi region, and the Tuareg, Sonni Ali left behind an empire that was well-structured and strategically positioned to control the trans-Saharan trade. His legacy is a complex one, characterized by both his military achievements and the brutal methods he employed to achieve them. His death in 1492 marked the end of an era, but the empire he expanded continued to thrive for a century after his passing. King Sonni Ali's life and reign remain subjects of both scholarly study and oral tradition, reflecting the enduring impact of his rule on the history of the Songhai Empire and West Africa.

In the land of old, where tales unfold,
Lived a king both fierce and bold,
Sonni Ali, the Songhai's pride,
With his wit, he took them for a ride.

From humble roots, he rose to power,
A leader for every waking hour.
With sword in hand and strategy keen,
He conquered lands like none had seen.

Timbuktu and Djenne, under his reign,
Echoed with victory, not without pain.
His methods harsh, his heart was steel,
Yet his vision, oh, so real.

Through the sands and rivers wide,
He rode with valor, never to hide.
Cavalry thundered, a force to behold,
As trade routes flourished, tales were told.

In the realm of faith, he stood apart,
Merging Islam with his Songhai heart.
Orthodox or not, his spirit pure,
His legacy, a tale to endure.

If Sonni Ali walked our world today,
What would he do, what would he say?
Perhaps he'd teach us to stand tall,
To strive for greatness, never to fall.

To blend our roots with modern times,
To rise above life's steep inclines.
With courage bold and wisdom true,
To make our dreams, our destinies, come through.

So let us learn from Sonni Ali's lore,
To march ahead, to seek for more.
To honor his memory, make him proud,
As black men rise, strong and unbowed.

King Muhammad Rumfa of Kano

King Muhammad Rumfa of Kano, reigned from 1463 to 1499, and is remembered as one of the most significant rulers in the history of the Kano Sultanate, now part of modern-day Nigeria. His rule marked a period of considerable wealth and opulence, which led to Kano's emergence as a commercial powerhouse in the region. Notably, Rumfa's reign was distinguished by substantial reforms that propelled the Sultanate to its zenith, particularly in terms of political influence and economic growth. Rumfa's legacy includes extensive infrastructural developments such as the expansion of the city walls, the construction of the Gidan Rumfa—a large palace named after him—and the establishment of the Kurmi Market, which became a hub for regional trade. His administrative reforms were equally transformative; he promoted slaves to governmental positions, a move that was unprecedented at the time. Furthermore, he was instrumental in the Islamization of Kano, urging residents to convert to Islam and building numerous mosques, including a significant one for Friday prayers.

The Sultan's efforts in governance also extended to the establishment of an Ombudsman for better administration and the formation of the "Taran Kano" (Council of Nine), which served as advisers and kingmakers. His influence on Islamic education was profound, with the arrival of the scholar Muhammad al-Maghili during his reign, who brought many Islamic books to Kano and left a lasting impact on the religious landscape of the region. Rumfa's policies and reforms laid the groundwork for the first Kanoan Empire under his grandson Muhammad Kisoki and initiated a period known as the "Rumfawa," which lasted until 1623. His era is considered by historians to be Kano's golden age in the pre-jihad era, and his name is still associated with greatness in the region, as evidenced by institutions like Rumfa College bearing his name.

In the heart of Kano's historic tale,
Lies King Muhammad Rumfa, whose reign did prevail.
From bustling markets to walls towering high,
His legacy echoes beneath the African sky.

In opulence and wealth, he held his sway,
Transforming Kano in his own regal way.
With Kurmi Market's hustle and Gidan Rumfa's grace,
He built a kingdom that time couldn't erase.

But 'twas not just gold that adorned his crown,
For his reforms and wisdom gained renown.
Promoting slaves to power, a bold decree,
Showing equality's true majesty.

In mosques and madrasas, he planted the seed,
Of Islam's embrace, a spiritual creed.
With al-Maghili's wisdom, the knowledge did flow,
Enlightening hearts with a heavenly glow.

In governance, he stood as a beacon bright,
Establishing councils to guide with insight.
With justice as his mantle, fairness his creed,
He ruled with wisdom, fulfilling every need.

Now, if Rumfa walked among us today,
What would he do? What would he say?
He'd champion justice, strive for the right,
And lead with compassion, a guiding light.

For in his footsteps, men today can tread,
With honor and virtue, no soul misled.
To emulate his grace, his noble art,
And make black men proud, in every part.

So let Rumfa's legacy forever inspire,
In every deed, let his spirit fire.
For in his reign, a golden age did unfurl,
A testament to greatness in this vast, grand world.

Robert Mugabe of Zimbabwe

Robert Mugabe was a central figure in Zimbabwe's history, serving as Prime Minister from 1980 to 1987 and then as President from 1987 to 2017. His early life was marked by education and teaching, which led to his involvement in nationalist politics against the white minority rule of Rhodesia. Mugabe's political journey began in earnest when he joined the Zimbabwe African National Union (ZANU) and became a prominent leader in the fight for independence. His efforts culminated in the Lancaster House Agreement, leading to the creation of a democratic Zimbabwe. As a leader, Mugabe initially pursued policies of reconciliation and development, focusing on education and health. However, his tenure was also marred by controversy, including economic challenges and human rights concerns. Despite these issues, Mugabe is remembered for his role in Zimbabwe's liberation and his impact on the country's political landscape.

In Zimbabwe's story, a chapter grand,
Stood Robert Mugabe, a man in command.
From teacher to leader, he rose with might,
A beacon of hope, in the liberation fight.

He started with books, in classrooms so bright,
Teaching young minds, guiding them right.
Then into the fray of politics, he stepped,
For Zimbabwe's freedom, his promise he kept.

With ZANU he marched, in the struggle so bold,
Against Rhodesian rule, his spirit unfold.
The Lancaster House was his crowning feat,
A new nation born, no longer in defeat.

As Prime Minister first, then President true,
He aimed for progress, with visions anew.
Education and health were his early quest,
To uplift his people, to give them the best.

But the road grew rocky, with challenges vast,
Economic woes and shadows cast.
Yet still, in the hearts of many, he's seen,
As a liberation hero, proud and keen.

Now imagine dear Robert, in our present day,
A sage old man, with wisdom to say.
Perhaps he'd be gardening, under the sun,
Or sharing his stories, when the day is done.

He'd tell young men, to be proud and stand tall,
To cherish their roots, and answer the call.
To lead with honor, to strive and to dream,
In every challenge, to find a bright gleam.

So here's to Mugabe, in memory sweet,
A complex figure, with legacy complete.
Men of today, look up and be proud,
Follow your dreams, and sing them out loud.

For in the tale of Zimbabwe, so rich and so vast,
Mugabe's impact, forever will last.
A mix of the good, the bad, and the bold,
A story of freedom, continuously told.

CONCLUSION

In conclusion, the poems in this book serve as a poignant reminder of the importance of good leadership in African countries. As we journey through the verses celebrating the legacies of iconic leaders such as Nelson Mandela, Ahmed Sékou Touré, Gamal Abdel Nasser, Thomas Sankara, Samora Machel, Kwame Nkrumah, Amílcar Cabral, Kenneth Kaunda, Ellen Johnson Sirleaf, among many others, we are reminded of the immense impact that visionary leadership can have on the trajectory of nations.

These leaders, through their courage, vision, and dedication to the welfare of their people, have shown us the way forward. They have demonstrated that with integrity, compassion, justice, socio-economic development, peace, and a commitment to good governance, African countries can overcome challenges and thrive.

As we look to the future, it is imperative that new leadership, particularly the youth, emulate the examples set by these trailblazers. They must strive to embody the principles of servant leadership, accountability, and inclusivity. By doing so, they can pave the way for a brighter, more prosperous future for the African continent.

This book of poems is not just a collection of words but a call to action. It is a call for our youth and future leaders to think deeply about the future of Africa and make conscious decisions to become effective and good leaders for the betterment of our continent. Let us heed this call and work together to build an Africa where all its people can thrive and prosper.

The End